Makin' Lemonade: A Guide for Choiceful Living

25th Anniversary Edition

Keri FitzPatrick, M.S.

Well-Being One (A division of Advanced Training & Consultancy) Littleton CO

Copyright © 2019, 2025 Keri FitzPatrick

All rights reserved.

No part of this publication may be reproduced, stored in a retrieval system, or transmitted in any form or by any means, electronic, mechanical, photocopying, recording, scanning or otherwise except as permitted under Sections 107 or 108 of the 1976 United States Copyright Act without the prior written permission of the publisher/author. Requests may be made to the publisher at wbochoice@gmail.com Short, limited quotes may be used in educational and/or professional publications with accurate and specific attribution to the author.

Limit of Liability/Disclaimer of Warranty: The publisher and the author make no representations of warranties with respect to the accuracy or completeness of the contents of this work and specifically disclaim all warranties, including without limitation warranties of fitness for a particular purpose. No warranty may be created or extended by sales or promotional materials. The advice and strategies contained herein may not be suitable for every situation. This work is sold with the understanding that the publisher and author is not engaged in rendering medical, legal, or other professional advice or services. If professional assistance is required, the services of a competent professional person should be sought. Neither the publisher or the author shall be liable for damages arising herefrom. The fact than an individual, organization, or website is referred to in this work as a citation and/or potential source of further information does not mean that the author or publisher endorses the information, the individual, organization, or website provide or recommendations they/it may make. Further, readers should be aware that internet websites listed in this work may have changed or disappeared between when this work was written and when it is read.

Image attributions: All images, unless otherwise attributed, have been created by the author using the online tool Canva. In some cases public domain images have been used and are cited as such. The combination of images from the Canva website and labeled in this work are intellectual property of the author and fall under copyright.

Author: Keri FitzPatrick, M.S.

Published by: Well-being One (A division of Advanced Training and Consultancy, LLC) Littleton, CO

Contact: wbochoice@gmail.com

ISBN: Print Copy 978-0-9676492-1-4   Electronic Copy 978-0-9676492-2-1

Contents

Introduction 1
The journey continues!

1. Navigating Your Discovery Pathway 6

2. Physical 15
   Embrace the process--it's yours to do with as you choose. As YOU choose. As you CHOOSE.

3. Emotional 47
   Your willingness to feel will determine your layers of experience within yourself and those you care about.

4. Intellectual 65
   Wellp, here's a big topic.

5. Social and Relational 76
   In the sweetness of friendship, let there be laughter and the sharing of pleasures. For in the dew of little things, the heart finds its morning and is refreshed -- Khalil Gibran

6. Spiritual 97
   Seeking meaning in something greater than ourselves takes many forms.

7. Educational and Occupational 101
   The only place success comes before work is in the dictionary -- Vince Lombardi

8. Financial and Legal 111
   It's up to you how complicated you make these areas -- your actions are quite tangible in the past, present, and planning for your future.

9. Volitional 117
   Embodied strength starts with embodied awareness. -- Pamela Meyer, Staying in the Game

10. Go.Be.Do. 124
   Every day holds opportunity.

11. What's in the Works? 129
   Oh yes, there's more to the journey ahead!

Introduction

The journey continues!

Welcome to the 25th Anniversary Edition of *Makin' Lemonade: A Guide for Choiceful Living*, I'm so glad you're here!

August 2024 — What is it like to take the next steps? To look out ahead and say, *Here we go* then launch into the next thing? The next set of thoughts, ideas, feelings? Well, we are here and I promise the next leg of this journey is full of **Insight-Based Learning (IBL)** exercises, tons of references for your own further research and new topics integrated into the Eight Life Areas. From this point forward I'll reference the original book as *Lemonade*.

I thank you for your input and suggestions over the years, decades in all actuality, because your requests for this type of content is what sparked *Lemonade*. And speaking of that, I'm including some of the original introduction here though I've made significant changes within the chapters. Whereas *Lemonade* was a guided journal this 25th Anniversary Edition is at once a book, a guide, and a set of cascading exercises that build on the **IBL and Discovery Pathway** I've developed based on research, clinical practices and intentional models.

As in everything, what you put into your discovery process will determine what you get out of it. There is **much to be curious about** as you look at your own behavioral and decision-making patterns . As you peel back the layers of your emotional life areas you will likely have the occasional "aha" moment, and as you see the interconnectedness of these elements you will likely feel a sense of clarity in each chapter. This book is for you if you are just a tiny bit curious and you like to learn...

Please write in, mark up, color on and put tabs all over your book, you'll get a deeper experience by being actively engaged. Allow your curiosity to lead you into new learning. Your discovery

and relationship with your thoughts, feelings, beliefs, attitudes and behavior(TFBAB) is what I've come to call *The Weave of It All*.

Discovery comes through your courage to seek new answers, to be vulnerable and authentic, and your commitment to growth. The techniques are built for forward movement through reflection, honest responses, and what I coined as Insight-Based Learning (IBL) back in 1995 (there's a vague World War II era reference to a writer named Kohler, however, my recent research shows my terminology to still be my own). Here's a summary of how I described the process: IBL is designed to be **accomplished through various reflection exercises contained in this *work*book and more broadly by your follow-up with recommended reading and other resources.**

I've been plaintively asked, "Yes, but **HOW** do I do this?" and the answer is by following the **Discovery Pathway and paying attention** to what it is you want to gain clarity on and an understanding of in your life. For example, if you want to better understand why and how you get into certain kinds of relationships, first define what the elements of those relationships are and what it is that attracts you to the people in them. By using the **question and self-assessment** models you'll work your way to clarity and decisions on what to do next. Where you need help understanding options for new behavior there are multiple citations and resources for you to go to **find a fit** with your willingness, ability, values and motivation cycle.

The word *work* was italicized in the original edition, fortunately journalized discovery, aka workbooks, have become much more common these days and so we no longer have the need to press that point. What I will press upon you is that **every person's process is their own unique journey**. I believe in your self-efficacy, your ability to develop and grow into your goals, and your self-determination as you find insights that motivate change in your life areas. **Insight + Action = Outcomes.**

I quote several authors, podcasters, philosophers, psychologists and other professionals in the sciences of human development and change process. I have also listed resources in each life area, no need to search an index (there isn't one) for references. One of the first notations comes from Gestalt Psychology (Fritz & Laura Perls, primarily recognized as two of the earliest practitioners in the 1940s) where **gestalt** literally means the sum is greater than its parts (Cambridgedictionary.com). Why so much focus on pioneers in psychology? Because their methods are based on creating self-awareness through discovery and allowing the client to own their insights. **Gestalt is a whole that can always be added to, there is room for growth and determining how much something is going to play an active role in your life.**

Insight-based Learning (IBL) combines the early philosophy of understanding self-directed growth and what is known as cognitive behavioral techniques (CBT). Rather than give you a history lesson on the development of **CBT** here's a synopsis found on Wikipedia: "Cognitive behavioral therapy focuses on challenging and changing cognitive distortions (such as thoughts, beliefs, and attitudes) and their associated behaviors to improve emotional regulation and develop personal coping skills." Other approaches included in the formulation of IBL and the Discovery Pathway include Dialectical Behavior Therapy (DBT) and Acceptance and Commitment Therapy (ACT).

> **So there you have it, the foundation of IBL comes from a holistic, person-centered place where thoughts, feelings, beliefs and attitudes that lead to behavior are discovered through guided exercises. Your own desire to consider and commit to change or sustaining behavior is your measure for success—How much do you want something and what are you willing to do to make a change or maintain your level of functioning? Simple, yet not easy.**

I've updated my description of the **Discovery Pathway** to this: **curiosity leads to awareness** that there is something to seek out, in the process of **seeking information** we base **understanding** on previously learned content and we build **meaning** which then leads to **intention and motivation to act on** a new thought or behavior, the **results are self-assessed** as something to **keep, modify or toss** depending on your estimate of how well it fits for you. **Beliefs** and **attitudes** are created through the weave of **experience/actions**. Then the pattern starts all over again with, **"I wonder if..."**

I titled *Lemonade* not only on a handy metaphor, but on my real life experiences with my grandmother as I tried to make sense of whatever *thing* was bothering me at one point or another along my path mostly before I left for college. During those times Grandma would have me join her at the kitchen table with a beautiful glass pitcher of homemade lemonade and she'd ask "what's buggin' you?" She always listened like a pro, gave little advice and never failed to provide endless love and encouragement. I dedicated this book to her then and I do so again today. I now have an even deeper realization of how much she taught me when she'd take me outside to the garden to "have a look around" and ask what I thought a certain tool might do or how the sun affects growth patterns. So there you have it, tools, growth and patterns are what this book is all about.

Disclaimer: If you are in crisis call the National Crisis Hotline at 988 or call a local crisis center, or 911. Take action for yourself and your life to <u>move through</u> your crisis. A crisis is temporary even though you might not feel that way in the moment, you matter, if you are in crisis, reach out to someone. If you are having a mental health crisis and you call 911, ask for a Crisis Intervention Teams (CIT) trained officer.

If you would like information on mental health programs and support in your area try the National Alliance for Mental Illness (NAMI) https://www.nami.org/

This workbook is not intended as medical advice or psychotherapy, any action you take you have sole responsibility for and if you need medical or psychiatric attention, please seek it for your own health and well-being.

This workbook takes time and varying degrees of focus, rest and resetting. You are likely going to be surprised by some of your discoveries, be sure to **celebrate your courage** on your journey. When I'm asked, I suggest that readers take a minimum of six months to complete the exercises. Also, complete is loosely defined. Once we get started on life changes we tend to keep going, we **weave threads** of all the life areas when we discover new pathways, and remember, the **weave is truly a *thing.***

The Eight Life Areas (abbreviated definitions):

1. **Physical** — Your body and its workings; your health and physiological reactions; your patterns of physical self-care and adornment.

2. **Emotional** — Your feelings and emotion fueled reactions and responses to stimuli/input; your inward messaging and outward expression of emotion as you relate it situationally.

3. **Intellectual** — Your information processing patterns and preferred learning styles; communication choices; intellectual stimulation and understanding of content; your drive to learn and work toward mastery and competency in meaningful ways.

4. **Social and Relational** — Your dynamic connections to and with other people at various levels of acquaintance, friendship, and, familial bonds.

5. **Spiritual** — Your belief in something greater than yourself which could include but does not

necessarily mean religion; your willingness to recognize an energy geared toward growth and hope.

6. **Educational and Occupational** (formerly listed as Vocational and Educational) — Your academic interests and value of learning that is combined with your values around work, employment, goal setting and meaningful tasks which may include volunteer activities.

7. **Financial and Legal** — Your relationship with money and spending patterns as well as legal engagements, concerns, and awareness.

8. **Volitional** — Your choices and self-determination as you understand them within the context of your decisions, values, and relationships that include all thoughts, feelings, beliefs, attitudes and behavior (TFBAB).

While arranged in this order each chapter has additional topics. I acknowledge that each chapter could be a book in itself — yet another reason to take the time you need to authentically do exploration and reflection.

My citations are my choice and are not requested by or financially related to any other entity. Unless otherwise noted, I have read, some I have engaged with and all I have intentionally cited because their content flows with Insight-Based Learning.

With regard to ableness I tried to be inclusive with my language and alternative text. The bottom line is this, please engage in IBL as it fits for you.

Any errors are my own, I welcome input and corrections at wbochoice@gmail.com

This book is protected by US and international copyright law, all rights belong to Keri FitzPatrick (2025). Refer back to the copyright page for more details.

Chapter One

Navigating Your Discovery Pathway

HAVE YOU EVER USED a journalized style of **self-discovery** before? If so, you know there are questions and suggestions for action on whatever topic the journal/workbook is about. In this workbook we cover a wide range of topics, each one moves incrementally deeper for awareness and meaning-making as preparation for planning, action and sustained new thoughts, feelings, beliefs, attitudes and behavior (TFBAB). If you haven't tried this kind of discovery this might feel new and maybe a bit daunting at first. My advice is to hang in there and go slowly, each chapter builds on the previous so you have a chance to learn as you go forward.

If you decide you'd like to practice this kind of work with books that are more focused in one life area I encourage you to seek titles that reflect the information you want, then, come back to this workbook for greater meaning-making once you've established a baseline of your own. As always, **your journey is your own**, you choose what you'd like to try and how you go about it.

Here are some examples of other authors work that might resonate with you:

- TableTopics *Happiness* Prompted Journal (2025)

- *Gratitude Journal: 110 Inspired Writing Prompts to Amplify Your Gratitude and Positivity* (2024)

- *Who Moved My Cheese*, S. Johnson (1998)

- *Chicken Soup for the Soul*, Jack Canfield (multiple topic titles).

- *The Let Them Theory*, Mel Robbins (2024)

When you engage in journal work it's best to find a place where you are physically and emotionally comfortable for at least thirty minutes. Time flies by when you are in a self-discovery process, set a timer if you need to get up and go someplace at a certain time because you'll find yourself engrossed in your process. Usually no more than two hours is plenty for one sitting. Our brains need time to process the input, you'll have feelings popping up to notice and you may need to determine what, if anything needs to be done other than just letting it all soak in for a bit.

Here's a visual of the IBL **Discovery Pathway** described in the Introduction. **Discovery is rarely if ever a linear experience,** you'll be all over the map at times, go with your process and embrace your insights.

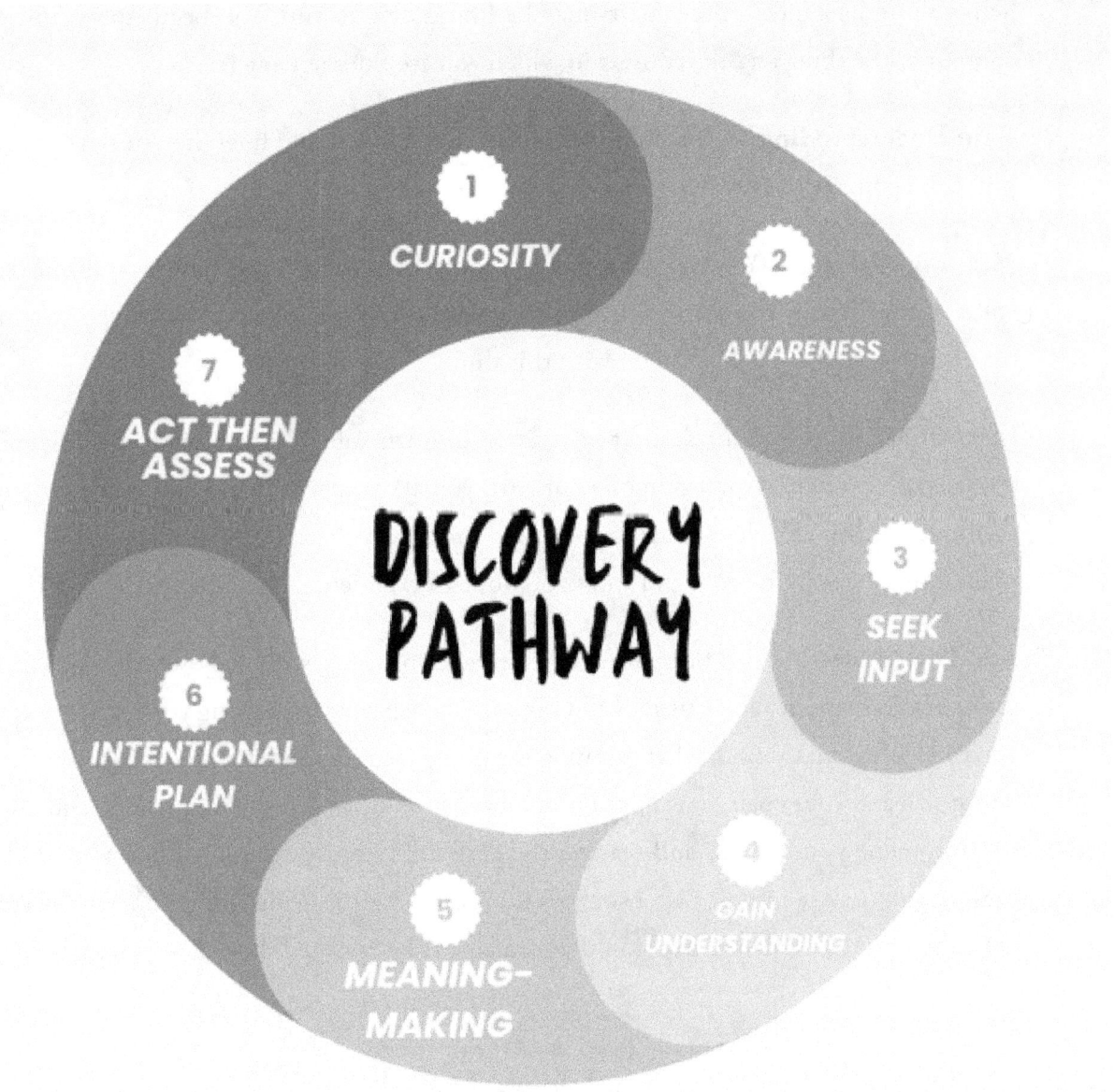

The Discovery Pathway:

1. **Curiosity** — You wonder about something, you feel inquisitive and maybe a little excited to see or learn something new.

2. **Awareness** — You notice an emotional and/or intellectual relationship to thing you are curious about; you desire more information and/or experience of this thing

3. **Seek Input** — You engage with this thing, you notice parts of it that you may have seen before to

help you understand it, other parts may be brand new to you. You begin to organize the content of the thing and the context in which you are experiencing it.

4. **Gain Understanding** — You start to connect the elements and how they work together or not; this is similar to assembling puzzle pieces to create a whole.

5. **Meaning-Making** — You add your understanding, values, and expectations of the of the elements. You identify connections to known and new information that creates your readiness for decision-making on what to do with this thing.

6. **Intentional Plan** — Your desire to continue to learn something about this thing and to engage with it requires intention on your part; you ask yourself "What do I want to do with or about this thing?" which leads to your need for concrete steps. You decide what you want to do, how you want to do it and what you hope to experience.

7. **Act Then Assess** — You put your steps into action which will likely set off a mixture of thoughts, feelings, beliefs, attitudes and potentially behavior. Following your primary action you then assess that action: what meaning is coming from discovering this thing, what can it do for you and your goals, how might it be a barrier to other desired experiences, and on and on. You refine your actions and reassess the desirability of this thing—if you want to keep it as useful, tuck it away for later, or toss it. You've identified the thing as having personal meaning or not and made a decision that can always be revisited should you choose.

And so revolves the Discovery Pathway — take a minute to write about something simple that fits this model so you have a clear understanding of it. Here's a short example to get you started: Imagine a time you saw an object that you didn't immediately recognize, you moved toward the object **and then what happened**: (write out what you did then write the name of which step in the Discovery Pathway that fits that step through all seven steps)

Trigger Warning: As mentioned already, your work might bring up some feelings and memories you weren't consciously aware of or might prefer not to look at and deal with. Triggers happen on the emotional and reactive level — we feel alarmed and threatened, we might re-experience an event (usually the experience is the leftover emotion from the event) and it's important to remember the event is in the past, not real in this moment in time. Triggers tell us there is work to be done. Grounding exercises are a great way to get through a trigger, I'll list a couple here and provide a link. If you have triggers that you are not managing, I recommend you seek help with them and the related content being triggered. Seeking therapy is a great self-care practice.

https://www.healthline.com/health/grounding-techniques#physical-techniques

Grounding Practice 1: When you feel triggered and need to "**settle down**" and get back into the here and now—

- Take a deep breath and notice your exhale for 3 seconds

- Repeat this 3x

- Feel with a solid object like your desk, your chair, the couch wherever you are right now and list out the elements of that object, i.e.

    - "The couch is fabric, it has a design on it that I can feel with my fingertips, it has squares and swirls." Or,

    - "The desk is wooden and it feels cool to the touch, there is a ridge on the edge, I can place both palms right here on my desk and feel the coolness."

- Then go back and do the 3 breaths again

- Assess by asking, "How am I feeling, do I need more breathing and grounding right now?"

- Continue intentional breathing — If you want to try something different, move to Grounding Practice 2. NOTE: If you are in a panic or anxiety attack, call a provider, a friend or if need be, emergency medical assistance.

Grounding Practice 2: When you feel **the need to move around** to physically and emotionally reset—

- Slowly and intentionally get up or move from where you are and go to a safe space where you can stretch your limbs without knocking into anything

- Notice the tension in your body, where do you feel most tense or constricted? Place your hands on that spot and notice the warmth from your hands soaking into the tense, constricted part of your body.

- Breathe in for a count of 3, breathe out for a count of 3

- Repeat the breaths, in for 3, out for 3

- In for 3, out for 3

- In for 3, out for 3

- Notice a soothing feeling in your body at the point where it was formerly constricted, allow it to relax

- Breathe in for 3, out for 3 and feel the tension melting away

- Repeat, in for 3, out for 3 breaths

- Place your hands on a solid surface like the floor or your desk, where ever you are standing or seated, find a solid surface to place your hands

- Breathe in for 3, out for 3

- In for 3, out for 3

- Feel your calmness, brush the air with your hands as though you are brushing out tiny bits of something you no longer need.

- Put your palms together and breathe in for three, out for three ending the final out breath with a burst of air to release the constriction.

If you can breathe in for 4 and out for 4 you'll get an even deeper release.

Grounding Practice 3: Engage in **intentional, repetitive** behavior

- Walk slowly for a minute, then change your method to heel-to-toe (match your toes to the heel of the foot you have in front) and walk like this for 5 minutes.

- Let your thoughts wander, concentrate on heel to toe, even say it out loud or in your head, just focus on the movement and intention of heel-to-toe.

- After 5 minutes, go back to slowly walking with a longer stride, arms at your sides for 2 minutes.

- Allow your mind to come back into the larger present, notice the room or area where you are walking, make note of items that surround you.

- Breath in and out 3x deeply.

- Return to what your were doing when you noticed you needed a little grounding break.

Other options for intentional, repetitive behavior include, but are not limited to: using a rowing machine for 10 minutes; walking around the block of your building or in a park; hand washing dishes (there's research on the calming quality of putting our hands in water).

IBL TOOLS & RESOURCES

- Understanding the IBL Process

- Other Works that use Journalized Methods

- **IBL Discovery Pathway © 2025**

- Trigger Warning

- Grounding Practices

Chapter Two

Physical

Embrace the process--it's yours to do with as you choose. As YOU choose. As you CHOOSE.

I'VE BEEN ASKED WHY physical is the first area I start with in *Lemonade*. On the one hand, it's the most tangible and we engage with our physical self every day, we present our selves to others in a physical form and we must maintain our bodies. On the other, it's one that causes a great deal of self-critical inward conversation and incessant striving to be better. Starting here is a solid foundation for all the discovery in this workbook. Give yourself time to work through the exercises, when you want to quit, take a break to reset, yet make a commitment to return to the work. As I've mentioned before, the workbook is written as a series of exercises, each one builds on learning from the previous set of questions and reflections. You will catch on to the flow of the questions if they don't seem obvious. Where there's a question **answer from where you are today**, how you feel, what you think, what you wish and hope and want and have. Here we go...

Physical. Physicality. Physicalness. All of these have related meaning, what do the words mean to you?

To assess this area respond to questions relating to your physical health overall, medical conditions, mental health conditions, hygiene, sleep, nutrition, exercise, sexual activity, manner of dress, makeup/adornment, body image, and, physical safety. Chapter One takes a very detailed approach to get your assessment lens focused, following chapters ask you to use your finely tuned lens and provide opportunities for adjusting your focus. As you look deeper from one area to the next you will discover the interrelated conditions and situations that are your *weave.*

My birthdate is: and today I am   years of age.

I was/was not born with a medical condition. If yes, what is the condition:

My medical condition plays a role in my life today by impacting:

My overall health, today, is considered(circle one or describe in detail): Poor   Fair   Good   Excellent by my <u>medical professionals</u> and I know this because:

<u>I consider</u> my overall health to be:

I have contributed to my overall health by (list behavior and attitudes that have caused you to gain/maintain your current level of health or lack of good health):

I am on prescription medication Yes/No and if so, I take my medication as directed   Yes/No because:

I take the following over the counter (OTC) medications and supplements for (list conditions, reasons, regularity):

I have an injury Yes/No

If yes, I attend physical therapy (if prescribed) Yes/No AND I follow through with my home-based exercises as prescribed Yes/No. I engaged at this level because:

I engage in self-care practices such as (massage, acupuncture/pressure, facials, etc.) for muscle and skin care:

I engage in physical activity for self-care reasons (list well-being practices such as yoga, and sports, dance, etc. specifically)

Being completely honest, which of the physical maintenance and physical movement items on my list do I **truly enjoy**, and why?

Being completely honest, which of the above items are more of a **chore** than a joy and why?

What would I miss if I ceased doing the items on the list that I do not enjoy?

What am I willing to change to create joy in one or more items (be specific with item name and change of activity).

When am I willing to start this change?

What could I do today to make one change? Just one change.

What is my resistance about regarding this change?

> As you can see, the questions require reflection and an honest self-assessment. This is how your commitment to change begins, you look at where you are with a clear lens and determine what you want to change, how you will go about it and how you will know you are in your change process. We'll get to more on the science of the change process in the next few pages, notice your feelings right now, as you look at the questions, **where are you feeling sure of your answers as tangible facts** and where are you not so sure? Mark the items where you are sure so that they stand out as differentiated from the not so sure responses.

What do you think your level of comfort means in both the tangible fact areas and the areas where you feel less sure or comfortable?

Self-talk matters, if you wrote a judgmental statement, please change it to be merely a statement of fact using **behavioral** (what you did rather than judging what you did) words. Words matter, Now is the time to start **practicing kind statements.**

Danna's Story

Danna read Makin' Lemonade shortly after it was published in 1999. She contacted me through a mutual acquaintance to discuss the content of the first chapter and to be sure I understood how hard it is for a person to look themselves in the mirror (an exercise in the book about seeing yourself in the mirror). Literally. Danna opened up our call with: I read your book. I know you must not have ever had a body image problem because you would not have asked anyone to look in the mirror if you did. I skipped this chapter altogether and worked on another one so I could just think for a while but that chapter referenced the first one so I had to go back. I don't like how you did that. It took me three months of going back and forth before I could get through the first chapter. It is hard to change how I see myself. I get it now why you started with physical, it's just that is my greatest area of pain if I was to just be honest.

And so, over the next several months I heard from Danna as she worked through the rest of the workbook and I learned that she had taken action to address her now diagnosed diabetes and related weight concerns. She had avoided going to the doctor for years because she did not want to get on the scales and be shamed for her weight and dietary habits. She used the word shamed. In fact, she was the one making harmful statements to herself and she was genuinely surprised when she was referred to a specialist with a dietician and coach. I saw Danna a few years ago and her transformation was wonderful. She had lost some weight, was going to water aerobics and walking regularly, had a new partner and was on medication as prescribed for her diabetes. Her smile was genuine when she said Makin' Lemonade gave her the push she had been avoiding. My response to her was that the workbook was a vehicle, she did the pushing and hard work toward lasting meaningful change.

The work you move into next is about body image. Much has been published in the twenty-five years since *Lemonade* first came out. The exercises that follow are cognitive behavioral technique (CBT) methods mentioned in the introduction. The exercises are not intended to be therapeutic interventions alone, however you may certainly want to use your discoveries in sessions with a therapist. Workbooks such as this are meant for self-assessment, self-awareness and action planning. Behavioral change agents may also use these exercises as tools with clients.

If you think you may have an eating disorder please see the website below for assistance, it could be a life saving move on your part. If you feel you are in crisis, call 988 or 911 to ask for help.

https://www.nationaleatingdisorders.org/

Over the past decade there has been MUCH ado on body image particularly as it relates to body positivity and body shaming on social media sites. We're going to start with some basics and then get to the dynamics of perception and the rationale for holding onto certain beliefs and attitudes.

Body image is defined as how you think and feel about your physical appearance.

In your mind's eye, or in front of a mirror, look at your clothed body.

a) What do you notice first? (make a note of self-talk, we'll come back to that in a bit, just jot it down and let it go for the moment, that's called **creating a parking lot**)

b) Where do you look next, and what do you notice about this area? (use the parking lot for self-talk)

c) Once again, move to the next area, what is the path your eye takes and how did you decide to take this path?

Notice the comments in your **parking lot**, what are the themes and patterns? Circle positive, kind, friendly statements you made about yourself.

What is left in the parking lot?

Looking at the list, what is the **ratio of kind self-talk to unkind** self-talk?

How do you feel about your self-talk as you look at it now?

What would you say to a friend, teen or a child who made the same comments about themselves?

You know where we are headed here, so, make the leap, **speak to yourself with kindness and intention** about just one of the judgmental things you put in the parking lot. Write your new self-talk here:

This is an introductory exercise in body image work. Introductory and not all that easy, right? Most people have something they want to change or in their own judgement, improve. The point here is two-fold: let go of the judgment, it does absolutely nothing for you but cause harmful feelings, and, if the area is something that can be changed, create a reasonable plan to make changes.

A Story About My Feet

When I was in second grade my aunt bought me some of those old fashioned clip on roller skates so I could ostensibly glide about on them. I watched people on skates on TV and I wanted that sense of freedom. The first challenge was figuring out the whole contraption, yet, where there's a will...Next, my skating area was the garage floor at my aunt and uncle's house. Barely two car widths with 4 giant seams in it. After a few small steps and low velocity crashes, I got the hang of balancing and stepping over the cracks, I could quickly get the skates on and off and I could adjust the size to fit whatever shoes I had on. That's where things got weird. The input from the adults varied from, Hmmm, we didn't know if you could do that...you aren't all that coordinated but you seem good at this... To, We hope the rest of your body grows into those feet because those skates have to last a while.

Please feel free to roll your eyes as you read about my early roller skating experience. Then, why might your reaction be eye rolling? What did you hear in the comments from adult family members in this story about body image? There are only three lines of narrative regarding the adults, and yet... This is what I mean about looking at where we learn self-talk, and self-judgment.

As an aside, I became a really good roller skater. Now, back to you.

What is your input, in this case, **comments and information sharing**, on the area you've selected to look at? Input is the collection of self-talk, comments from friends, family, media — including social media, professionals like physicians, trainers, instructors, etc. Who is saying what about this area you have selected as your focus? Write it here:

Now, given all the input, what is **reasonable? Useful? Kind?**

What are you willing to let go of? Mark it out if it **does not serve you**, if it is not kind, mark it out and let it go.

Take a few minutes, actually **set a timer for 7 minutes** and write all that comes to your mind now on this area that you have selected to work on, just let free associations and thoughts ramble and write them here.

No need to judge your writing, or analyze the written word, the point at this very moment is to ask yourself: How do I feel right now, in this very moment?

After completing this set of exercises, take a break from your work in this area. Your break can be as short as 15 to 30 minutes or as long as a few days, you decide. You've done more work in the last few pages than perhaps you have in a while regarding body image and the areas that are triggered by this work. Leave space here to come back and jot things down as bits of insight seep in. AND one more thing, be kind to yourself during your break — drink water, breathe deeply, appreciate something in nature or your surroundings and **say out loud** the positive self-talk you created earlier. You are worth it.

So, how long of a break did you take? Why?

Here's a useful quote and segue from a Therapist Aid sheet created in 2021 titled *Body Image Discussion Questions*   https://www.therapistaid.com/therapy-worksheets

"You can develop a more rounded body image by focusing on your body as a whole, rather than just appearance. Think about your unique qualities, such as strength, gracefulness, or resilience. Or, consider specific functions your body serves, such as fighting off disease, or getting through a tough day. **What do you appreciate about your body?**"

Please write your answer here:

If/when you feel ready, try the same set of exercises (all of them in this section, to this point) either in your mind's eye, or without clothing. Note what changed and write that here:

And now, what kindness are you **extending to yourself?**

As you are aware, gaining insight is only the first part of change, there has to be action. Fritz Perls has been attributed with the famous quote, "Insight without action is elephant [poop]." So, it's time to look at making plans for **any** changes you may have decided to take on.

In short, action planning can be made simple and you've probably heard of SMART goals one place or another. SMART stands for the following and to keep it easy, I've added short definitions:

<u>S — Specific</u>   What is the exact thing you want to achieve, i.e. add one walk in the park each week

<u>M— Measurable</u>   What exactly will you do, by when and HOW

<u>**A — Achievable**</u>   Can this goal be done in the timeframe you set and by the methods you choose

<u>**R — Realistic**</u>   Is this goal something you specifically, with your current abilities can accomplish

<u>**T — Time Referenced**</u>   Is the time frame specific, i.e. by 12-15 or 4pm on Thursday

Apply the SMART model to your stated area of change, will it work?

What are potential barriers to getting moving on this goal? Make a list below of **external** (outside yourself) and **internal** (within yourself, your thoughts, feelings, beliefs, attitudes and behavior) that could be barriers.

After looking at your barriers list you may have realized that you have a good runway to making a change if it's stated in small, reasonable steps. If not, break it down farther, what is the very first thing that has to happen for you to have some success? Give that thing a very quick time frame, like, by 4pm TODAY.

If you found some larger barriers, circle the ones that are within your control. If you have barriers outside of your control you only have influence over them, and perhaps not much at that. You can only change your self... there will be reactions and responses by others if they notice and are somehow impacted.

Start with something small, doable and meaningful to you. Recognize your success and celebrate! Define and describe your success here:

By this point in your workbook you likely have noticed that you've been asked what you are willing to do differently. Next is a popular readiness for change model that's been used in allied health fields for decades, it's called the Stages of Change and was first offered up in addictions related textbooks four decades ago by Prochaska and DiClemente (Prochaska, J. O., & DiClemente, C. C. (1983). Journal of consulting and clinical psychology, 51(3), 390.) Stages and processes of self-change of smoking: toward an integrative model of change.

This model can be used for virtually any kind of change you are considering and you will start in the stage that fits your awareness level. Below is a stock image of the stages of change and I've provided very brief definitions.

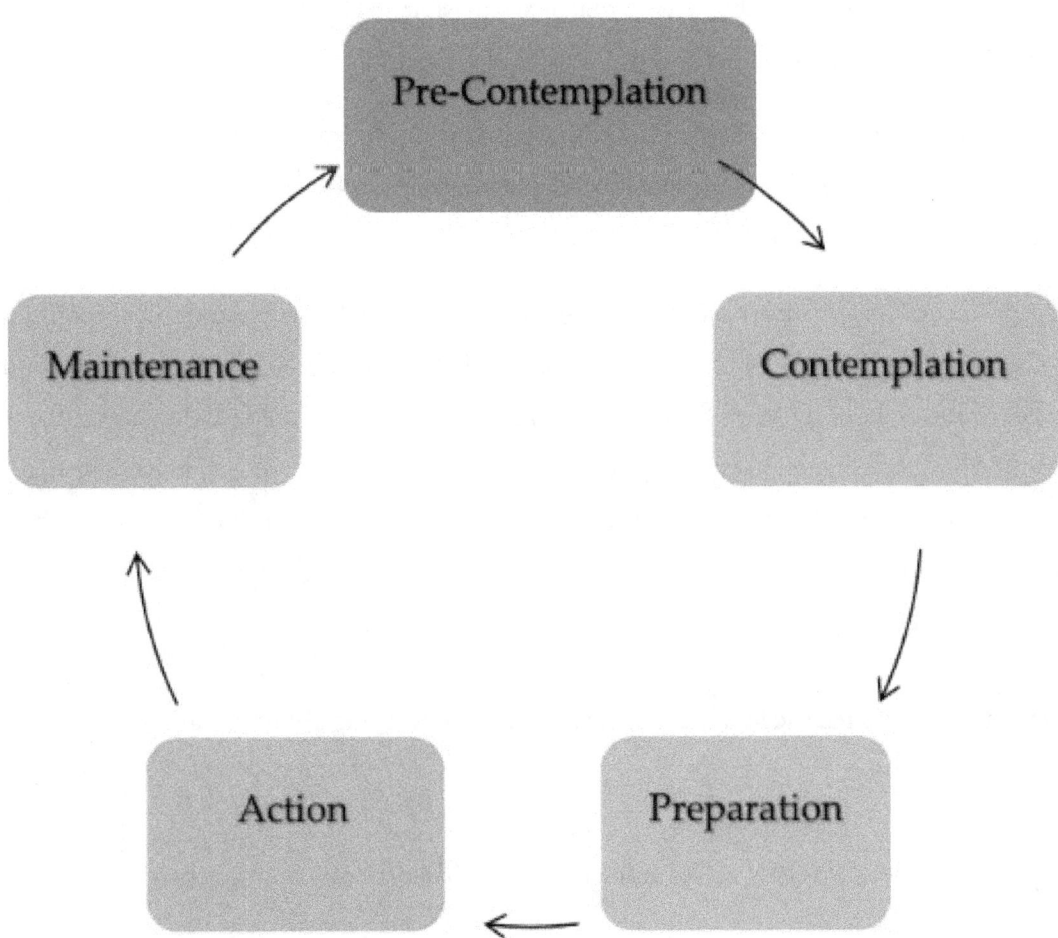

Precontemplation: You are not thinking about this as an issue, it's generally considered beyond your awareness, though others may have brought it up to you, you have regarded it as "not a fit."

Contemplation: You have begun to think about this issue, it may not even be the first time and likely is not the first time, you've thought about how this area affects you and perhaps others around you. You are thinking about it but not making any specific plans to do anything about it. You might be in the process of "seeing if anything happens" with it.

Plan/preparation: You've found a place to start, you have ideas about what could be changed and how to go about it. You've created SMART steps or goals and have dates on them. And yet, you could be stuck with a seemingly great plan but no action. This sounds a lot like, I'm going to; I'm planning to; When the time is right I have a plan to… Preparation is deeper than a to do list, it has intention, your intrinsic motivation starts to come into clearer focus here.

Action: Now you are working on elements of your plan in your life, you are trying new things, learning what works and what doesn't. You might have to stop, re-set, refine, re-do, whatever comes up, yet you are taking action.

Maintenance: You've now incorporated your change into daily living. It's not so much a constant thought in your conscious mind, you are doing this thing because that is part of you and how you go about your life. How long does it take to get here? Researchers disagree depending on the field they are in, the shortest amount of time has been suggested as 21 days of consistently engaging in the new behavior intentionally every day, usually multiple times in the day. Others say 60-90 days before maintenance can be defined. The main thing here is your commitment and consistency. Yes, you will struggle, that's part of change.

Many people struggle and relapse in patterns. What is the hardest thing about getting started for you?

The next question to be asked then, is, What stage am I in with my area I want to change?

By the way, pre-contemplation is beyond your awareness, so, you won't know it if you're in it.

You've identified your stage, how do you know you are in it? What are your thoughts, feelings, beliefs, attitudes and behavior (TFBAB) that tell you this is your spot?

Relapse happens. Relapse is a label of for a set of actions, it is **not to be judged**, the pattern is to be understood. It's common and bound to happen at some level in the TFBA BEFORE your behavior. Also, the stages are dynamic, not static, they change as you make decisions and try on changes.

Why do we get into this model? Because understanding the dynamics of your WHY regarding your changes is crucial for you to make a commitment to your change, to see it when it's happening, and to see relapse coming. The aim with this model is to give you a tangible place to plant your awareness flag and determine where to next.

Now that you have one model, you can look forward to others in this workbook. Models provide a **framework** to understand context, the relationship of one thing to a situation. **You choose the models** that speak to you and your process. That's called **resonance** and you'll know it when you experience it.

Switching focus a bit, the next topic under the broad awning of your physical life area is that of sleep. There are many, many dependent elements that come into play with sleep patterns, our value of sleep or rest, and the space we give it in our lives.

The University of Chicago has a long and storied history in sleep research. The link that follows is an excellent place to start to understand the necessity for sleep for all mammals.

https://news.uchicago.edu/explainer/how-sleep-affects-human-health-explained

If we start with the understanding, then, that we all need ADEQUATE sleep, we need to understand how we plan for and get that very important phase of each day (about 30% of our day) in place. Run a quick check-up with the following questions.

1. I sleep an average of _____ hours per night

2. I believe this is/is not adequate sleep for my own best health. Because:

3. I am a shift worker and have to sleep at differing times from my partner and/or I have to sleep during the day when the majority of my social connections are sleeping.

4. My sleep is restful when (describe the conditions):

5. I awaken frequently. If yes, for how long and what does it take to get back to sleep?

6. I fear sleeping because:

7. If yes to number 6, list what is currently under your control.

8. I take medication to help me sleep. Yes/No/Sometimes Because:

9. I drink/use substances to help me sleep. Yes/No/Sometimes The effect the next day is:

10. I use sleep as an escape from things happening in my life. Yes/No/Sometimes

11. If yes/sometimes to number 10, how long do you sleep or stay in bed not sleeping? How frequently does this happen?

12. I will put off sleep to get work or school assignments or social activities in place. If yes, how often?

13. I keep my smart phone by my bed Yes/No and I do this because:

14. I have difficulty removing myself from my electronic devices (phone/tablet/computer/TV/etc.) Yes/No because:

Look at your responses above, what patterns do you see?

Which questions did you have a difficult time answering and why?

Which item(s) do you think you'd like to change and why?

We need sleep to rest our minds and bodies. Research clearly indicates we need sleep to rebuild healthy immune systems. How are your sleep habits **impacting** your overall health?

As you've come to expect, we're going to segue again to a related topic: hygiene. You might feel surprised, but read on!

Hygiene is defined for our purposes as the general upkeep of your body: bathing, cleansing, brushing, oiling, lotioning, shaving, filing, and any other routine you do to keep all your body parts in working order and free of disease. The care and upkeep of body ornamentation counts here, too.

How are you doing in this area?

What is going on when you are not *feeling it* regarding doing all the "ings"?

Including hygiene, how are you feeling about your body right now?

What kindness can you offer yourself regarding your body? And when will you start?

Remember, if you are **avoiding answering** these inward looking questions, you've got something you are trying to perhaps protect — what is that? What are you **hanging onto that is blocking you from moving forward?**

How is this block serving you?

In what way does **meditation** play a role in your life?

Here's a bit of data that might help if you answered none/little. The excerpt below is from the Harvard Medical School website and was written in 2014. I mention the date because we've known this for years and years, yet it is still, in 2024 something that seems "out of the norm" and we have to wonder, Why is that? Why is something that is thousands of years old still considered unusual?

https://www.health.harvard.edu/staying-healthy/what-meditation-can-do-for-your-mind-mood-and-health-

"You can't see or touch stress, but you can feel its effects on your mind and body. In the short term, stress quickens your heart rate and breathing and increases your blood pressure. When you're constantly under stress your adrenal glands overproduce the hormone **cortisol**. *Overexposure to this hormone can affect the function of your brain, immune system, and other organs. Chronic stress can contribute to headaches, anxiety, depression, heart disease, and even premature death."*

You might find the site listed above quite useful, it holds all kinds of great research and the articles are built for information followed by action. **Remember, insight needs action**.

Next topic, nutrition.

The focus in this section will be mostly about patterns and your relationship with food and drink. Fuel. There are no recipes or diet recommendations. Numerous resources exist that delve into healthy food and supplement consumption. This section is about your thoughts, feelings, beliefs, attitudes and behavior (TFBAB) with food, beverages and other consumables. I've added an example next to a bullet to help you get started.

Make a bullet list of 5 words that describe your relationship with food. First just write the word then write about each word in a free flowing manner. Notice your TFBABs and circle patterns of descriptions you see in the list.

***Example**: *taste — I like the taste of certain foods, pesto sauce is a good example, I enjoy the layers of taste that I can identify and because it seems robust I feel full when I eat pasta with it on it, but I also really like it on turkey sandwiches to bring out the flavor. I like interesting food. If something doesn't taste good I feel disappointed and I won't eat it. I end up staying hungry sometimes because I was disappointed in my food and didn't have a back-up plan for what else to eat. Taste kind of motivates my eating habits — if I can't find something for lunch, etc. that I think will taste good I'll have juice or something to "fill the hunger gap" and move on. I don't want to waste time or energy or even caloric content on something that doesn't taste good. I realize this might not be a healthy approach since at least twice a week or more I skip a meal because I couldn't find something "tasty" to dine on. I also realize I could do meal planning, I really haven't put much effort into planning ahead.*

In the example above circle thoughts, feelings, beliefs, attitudes and behaviors in the statement. Now, try it out for yourself.

*

*

*

*

*

What surprises you in this exercise?

Behaviors, recommended in the healthy eating literature for a positive experience with food include: make eating about eating, that is, just eat and try not to do 1 or 5 other things at the same time; make a specific time to eat and try to stick to that schedule; create a full-o-meter by paying attention to when you feel full and when you continue to eat "for taste" or other desire; make a concerted effort to understand your own feeling of full and then eat to the point of feeling 80% full.

Of the list, which do you do regularly? Make notes here about your behavioral pattern.

What kind of food or beverage cravings do you have?

When do these happen?

What do you do about them?

How do you feel after you address a craving?

List your feelings right now as you are completing this section, what is coming up for you?

What is your self-talk? Is it true? Is it kind? How does it serve you?

Every five years the US government publishes dietary guidelines, you can find a comprehensive article on the why's and how's to integrate fuel giving food into your diet.

https://www.dietaryguidelines.gov/sites/default/files/2020-12/Dietary_Guidelines_for_Americans_2020-2025.pdf

Does your food intake provide fuel as you need it for your daily activities? Yes/No Why?

What is one change you are willing to make if you think you need to make a change? Just one change to get started. Remember, the goal is about **fuel,** not specifically your appearance.

If you binge and/or purge, it's time to get help. Now. Neither of these behaviors are about fuel, they are about an emotional and psychological condition related to a sense of control. Your life could be very much in danger if you are engaging in these behaviors. This workbook cannot address the scope necessary to impact binging and purging, please seek eating disorder specific intervention.

The Mayo Clinic based in Rochester MN and with clinics in Arizona and Florida has a very useful website,

https://www.mayoclinic.org/diseases-conditions/eating-disorders/in-depth/eating-disorder-treatment/art-20046234

There are specific red flags that may suggest an eating disorder, please see the Mayo Clinic site for those if you are curious. Make notes of any you engage in and the awareness that comes to mind. Look back at the **Stages of Change model, where might you fit with your awareness**? How do you know this?

And now, how do beverages play a role in your life? Make a few notes here of the types, frequency, any rituals or special events involved, and as you did above, add your feelings and thoughts about each.

And so, what have you noticed?

On a scale of 1-5, one being only a little honest, and 5 being straight up telling the truth, where did you land regarding your use of alcoholic, Non-alcoholic beer/liquor or marijuana/THC-infused beverages?

What message are you sending yourself here? Look at your answers to both primary questions in this section on beverages, what do you see? What is your relationship with beverages that cause an **altered cognitive and emotional state** that are not considered fuel for your body?

As you likely are aware, a continuum exists over a range of not problematic to is/has caused harmful impact to active, uncontrolled use. Terminology in addictions science and treatment changes from time to time, in the article at

https://www.verywellmind.com/substance-use-vs-substance-use-disorder-whats-the-difference-6385961 you can get a good sense of the different levels and impact of use behavior.

In the summary of the article cited above, there is a succinct description of the pattern and impact of use: *"Substance use is a broad term that encompasses every instance of using harmful substances such as alcohol, drugs, nicotine, cannabis, or prescription medications. Substance use disorder, however, is a medical condition that refers specifically to problematic use of these substances, to the extent that the person experiences negative consequences to several areas of their life."*

You can do an exhausting, not necessarily exhaustive, search for information about alcohol, as an example and you will find writers who state all alcohol use is harmful and that it is poison to the body that the body has to process and is thus harmed at each and every introduction into the body. You will find others who say X amount of drinks per day is not harmful. Here's the thing, ask yourself why you consume what it is that you consume and what you want that substance to do for you. **Be honest.** Make some notes below.

Help exists in many types of intervention and self-help support groups. Call 911 or 988 if you are in crisis right now.

I've referenced the Substance Abuse and Mental Health Services Association (SAMHSA) before, here is the landing page with many resources and links to find LOCAL resources for yourself:

https://www.samhsa.gov/find-support/health-care-or-support/support-group-or-local-program

Time for a summary of your work to pull it all together in this life area:

    1. What have you discovered about your behavioral patterns regarding problem or abusive intake of

food/beverages/supplements?

2. What steps have you taken as a result of these insights? **Write down who you have contacted and what action is related to that contact.**

Take a moment here for nurturing self-talk. You are doing hard work, **give yourself some grace and comfort.**

Self-soothing behavior is doing something for yourself that brings about a sense of calm(er) feelings, breathing exercises are a good example of self-soothing techniques.

- Try taking in three deep breaths and then letting them out slowly.

- Try that again and with the inhale breathe in for 3 counts, then exhale for 6 counts. This takes only a few seconds to do and the benefit is well worth it.

- There are many types of breathing exercises, sometimes it's called "breath work." Find something that fits for you and your level of willingness to actually practice, then add it in to your daily or hourly and as needed practice for a better sense of overall well-being. Check out *box breathing* and The Physiologic Sigh at https://www.inc.com/jeff-haden/stanford-neuroscientist-this-5-second-breathing-technique-is-fastest-way-to-reduce-anxiety-stress.html

One of my favorite sites for research-informed information is the Harvard Business Review at https://hbr.org/

https://hbr.org/2020/09/research-why-breathing-is-so-effective-at-reducing-stress

According to the article "*...different emotions are associated with different forms of breathing, and so changing how we breathe can change how we feel. For example, when you feel joy, your breathing will be regular, deep and slow. If you feel anxious or angry, your breathing will be irregular, short, fast, and shallow. When you follow breathing patterns associated with different emotions, you'll actually begin to feel those corresponding emotions.*

How does this work? Changing the rhythm of your breath can signal relaxation, slowing your heart rate and stimulating the vagus nerve whick runs from the brain stem to the abdomen, and is part of the parasympathetic nervous system, which is responsible for the body's rest and digest activities (in contrast to the sympathetic nervous system, which regulates many of our fight or flight responses). Triggering your parasympathetic nervous system helps you start to calm down. You feel better. And your ability to think rationally returns."

At this writing (November, 2024) there are several electronic applications (apps) available for smart phones and computer download that provide breath work, guided visualization and meditation, calming sounds, and gentle movement like chair yoga to slow down your breathing and provide space for focus in the present. Check out these options if you'd like to experiment with calming apps and provide yourself a gentle break to reset and recover even in short time frames.

Our understanding of exercise science and how it relates to our health continues to evolve. The insight-based work in this life area in the first edition of *Lemonade* reflected current trends, many are still applicable, and if we look way way back, say, not just over decades but millennia, we see the wisdom of thinkers and practitioners from early civilization and their understanding of the **need for movement** to have healthy bodies. Yoga comes to mind as does Tai Chi and other forms of meditation combined with movement. The mind-body connection is clear.

Take a moment here to write a description about **your relationship with movement.** Include things like how you feel when you move, what your thoughts about exercise include, how committed you are to any kind of movement and what you'd like to do differently. **Circle themes** in all these areas. Note barriers.

Take it a level deeper, what kinds of movement do you enjoy, what do you avoid and why?

Complete the sentence: I feel _____ when I _____ because_____.

Use the sentence structure above for feelings you enjoy and describe them with additional words that fuel your joy. Similarly, do the same with opposite feelings, what are the elements of not enjoying a type of movement? Why is this so? What thoughts go with both sides of this type of movement?

Science tells us about the natural feel good neurotransmitters that are released by moving our bodies. One online search at https://askthescientists.com/neurotransmitters/

outlines seven neurotransmitters and their relationship to our feelings as we move our bodies, as we eat and how we react to various kinds of stimuli. Understanding that concept of fuel, once again, is important for our insights on how we treat our bodies.

As mentioned previously, we can become "addicted" to certain feelings, the release of neurotransmitters and our pleasure center being "lit up" through activity. If we get into cycles like this we are prone to over using and potentially abusing an activity. The question to ask ourselves is why? What is it I am getting through this activity and how is it impacting my physical life area AND the other seven life areas? Remember, **the weave is real**.

Lynne's Story

Lynne was a graduate student when she first became unhappy with her body's contour. She had always been a student athlete and now grad school was too demanding to continue playing on multiple teams. Or even one team. She tried jogging and workout videos, but those didn't feel the same as being outdoors and on a team. She went to the pool to swim laps, that seemed to be more work than the outcome was worth. Her food intake was the same as college: pizza, salad, cheese and crackers, tacos, beers on Thursday's with other students in her program, buffalo wings while watching games on TV. As she got busier and less physically active her clothes started to fit tighter and she began her judgmental self-talk. The self-talk led into "I should" and "I ought" but no real change in behavior. Lynne started to feel generally displeased with her appearance and decided she looked "fat" and out of shape. She felt somewhat defeated and not herself.

While looking for a topic that was specific to females, exercise and body image that she might research for her thesis she found literature on using visualization in sports psychology. Lynne felt elated, this was a way to combine her interest in a technique for growth and for her to work out regularly.

As you might guess, Lynne truly applied herself to understanding the levels of visualization and varied weight lifting strategies. She also got "hooked" on her project past what could be considered healthy participation in her own thesis premise. Lynne obsessed about working out, she wanted the powerful feeling of an endorphin rush just as she got from sprinting as a soccer player in her recent past. She got the reward when she pushed harder and harder at weight lifting. She talked with other women in the gym, the ones who were there as often as she was, and learned they, too, wanted that pleasurable feeling they associated with success. Lynne joined a 24-hour gym so she could workout at any time in the day, she was there on average 3 hours a day, 6 days a week usually after class in the evening. Lynne traded a few hours of sleep for working out.

Lynne overtrained, her mother told her she was over built and "looked like a man." Lynne's mother said her muscle mass had gone from fit to over the top and large rather than proportional for her size. Lynne considered her mother's comments as judgmental and non-supportive.

The turning point came not from Lynne's completion of her thesis, but when two unrelated events forced her to unexpectedly evaluate and change her behavior. The IRS closed the gym and Lynne's mom sent a photo of Lynne taken when Lynne was home for the holidays three months earlier. In retrospect it was hard to say which event was most impactful. Lynne stared at the photo, her favorite red sweater was stretched over her shoulders and at her biceps, the bottom seemed shorter and hiked up because of the bulk of Lynne's upper body and arms. Lynne felt a sense of disbelief, she had not realized she'd made such a transformation. The gym being locked shut created a set of problems Lynne hadn't planned for and a cascade of feelings. How was she going to workout? What would she do with the time she spent at the gym? How was she going to find a way to feel good through exercise? In the immediate moments Lynne felt betrayed by the gym and confused about her own appearance. She truly hadn't realized the significant changes because she focused on the increments that seemed to be positive progress — yet as a whole, she'd done more than what she'd planned. What happened?

Lynne shared the photo with her roommate and explained that the gym was closed, that she was literally shut out. Lynne's roommate commented that she'd been wondering what it would take for Lynne to realize how much time she spent at the gym and what she was doing to herself. Lynne reacted with anger when her roommate challenged Lynne's beliefs, but, the photo was proof that yes, Lynne had taken her perception of herself too far. That in reality, perhaps she had harshly judged herself when she was in school and that she over reacted to correct something that could have been addressed with moderation. Lynne's roommate told Lynne she has a habit of going all out rather than looking for a middle of the road approach, and while that is often good, perfectionism really is a harsh set of beliefs and self-talk.

Lynne agreed she'd take a step back and evaluate how she got here, she had started a journal for her workouts and she could switch it up to include her thoughts and motivation. She added cross-training and muscle lengthening exercises to reduce the bulk. Lynne shared that after the first three months of her new routine she felt she was being more holistic and calmer in her approach, which actually felt better than she had over the past 18 months. Lynne joined a women's recreational soccer team for fun on the weekend and social connection, she moderated her weightlifting to focus on health rather than building, and generally stopped competing with herself for an unknown goal and level of recognition that she never was able to define.

Something to consider: **How you take care of your body reflects** your sense of your body's value. What are you doing to show it care, what are you doing that seems uncaring or too tough on it? Why?

Time to move into talking about sex. Sexuality, sensuality, libido, sexual activity and reproduction are all related but certainly not synonymous. The website https://www.endocrine.org/patient-engagement/endocrine-library/hormones-and-endocrine-function/reproductive-hormones

contains information about the hormones related to sex drive and reproductive systems for men and women.

Our focus in this workbook is on the activity you engage in, your motivation and the results. You might be feeling really uncomfortable right now thinking about writing down your sexual and intimate activity. Take a calming breath, this is not about recounting your history, the insights you might uncover will be related to what is working, what's not and what you might want to change.

Start with this list for baseline building:

1. I currently engage in sexual activity with another person(s). Yes/No

2. For me, sex is about:

3. For me, the difference between sex and intimate touch is:

4. What I want in a relationship regarding sex and/or intimate touch is:

5. There are times when I am not interested in sexual activity — those times are:

6. There are times when I am not interested in intimate touch — those times are:

7. I feel/believe I have been coerced into sex and/or intimate touch. Yes/No   I feel _____ as I answer this question right now because:

Take a break here for a few minutes or longer at this juncture, what do you need to self-soothe and remain in a balanced emotional space as you complete the baseline questions?

If you are in crisis at this moment call 988 or 911 and take action for yourself. Call 800-656-4673 for the national sexual violence hotline, you can go to online.rainn.org to find several resources and a link to the chat line at https://rainn.org/resources

Returning to your physical sexual experiences, the question is now what about sex do you enjoy, what would you like more of, and how will you endeavor to have that element more frequently in your sex life?

In your opinion, how healthy is this element for you? i.e. is it risky and possibly harmful, is it about gaining more intimacy, is it about feeling more fulfilled?

The questions above are places to begin your discovery, this section is about finding your baseline, looking at your patterns and checking in on a realistic basis about your sexual and/or intimate behavior.

As with every section, the overarching question for you to ask yourself is this, How does this serve me?

Now, a few questions about health and disease, again, at the baseline level.

1. I have a sexually transmitted infection or disease (STI, STD) or have had one in the past. Yes/No

2. This condition affected me by (list the associated health conditions, need for medication, etc.)

3. I feel _____ about my condition.

4. I use protection from disease by: and I use/don't use contraceptive methods because:

5. I engage/do not engage in self-pleasuring activity because:

6. My sexual organs/genitalia have been harmed by myself and/or other persons by (type of activity):

We'll take a moment here for you to gather your thoughts and feelings as you've been answering some potentially uncomfortable questions. The next question is important for your safety. As you consider your answer please know that honesty with yourself is the place to begin. Only you can decide if and when to take action and what that action might be. Below are some resources to consider.

7. I have been or am currently in physical danger of sexual violence or intimate partner violence : Yes/No

The national hotline for domestic violence is available 24/7 365 days a year, they have Spanish speakers, and can be reached several ways.

Text HOME to 741741 in the United States

Go to https://www.thehotline.org/

Reaching out is a first step, you will be asked what you think you need and nothing will be forced upon you. The first thing to ask for is information so that you can make informed decisions.

Call 911 or 988 for **emergency** help.

Again, take a break here to make sure you have answered the baseline questions. What are you feeling and thinking as you look at your answers?

If you need to reach out to a professional due to the answers above or your experiences, please take that action that fits best for you. This workbook is about finding healing pathways, put yourself in the position of self-care, not self-harm or allowing harm by others. **You have options**. Call 911, 988 or 800 656 4673 for immediate assistance.

As we transition toward the end of this first chapter the next topic is definitely lighter in intensity than those just completed, yet, for many people it represents how they feel **seen in the world** and within cultures. We're going to look at your mode of attire and adornment.

Style — it would take an anthropological and sociological course to cover the essence of style in various cultures and periods of time. I toured through dictionary.com to provide something useful here and really, the bottom line is this: Style is a manner of presenting yourself that you see as your "brand" or identity by selecting types of adornment. Ha! Helpful? Maybe. Here are a few other words that have stuck around over decades so we can try those: classic; on trend; athleisure; sporty; comfort first; business casual; elegant; designer/high fashion; logo and bespoke; goth; carefree; etc. You can search types of style if you want to narrow it down and give yours a label. The value of style is something that is learned and decided upon, consider your *style* and why you wear what you wear.

Define your style of dressing today:

How has your style changed over the years and what influenced the changes?

How much do you think about your clothes, jewelry, makeup, hair, and appearance?

If you were to say your manner of dress/attire gives off a statement about you, what is that statement?

Does this statement change with situations? If so, how?

What do you enjoy about your style?

What's difficult with your style?

What messages have you received from others about your manner of dress/style/appearance?

How much do you value those messages?

Complete this sentence: I feel best when my appearance is_____.

I have piercings and tattoos Yes/No

Those adornments mean (fill in the blank)   to me and send the message of   to others.

We send all kinds of non-verbal messages, overall, what message does your style send to those who know you, and, farther out on the social circles, to those who don't know you well?

What, if anything would you like to change about your outward appearance?

How would you do this in the short-term?   Is there a longer-term goal to set?

Looking back over your answers regarding your outward appearance, **what does it say about your inward experience?**

What does your appearance say about how you take care of your health and your body?

What is one action, **in the practice of self-care,** that you can do a bit more of that would be healthy and healing for your body — that you can do today?

As mentioned above, we are transitioning from one life area to the next. The insights you've gained in this first chapter may be substantial and impactful. There is no time limit on the workbook, it's your journey to embark upon as you choose. You've used and perhaps learned a few new techniques for inward reflection and action planning.

Truly, the key to making a change is to find an action you are willing to engage in, try it out, refine it to make it workable for you and fit your goal, then commit for a few weeks to **give the behavior a chance to become a sustained part of you**.

Go back through this chapter as often as you like, put it down for a while and work on the next one, all of it is up to you. Insight is a process as is creating your own understanding of choicefulness. Make a few notes below on your own process and how you envision, today, your **pathway to choiceful living** — while this chapter focuses on the physical life area, clearly emotions and thoughts are a big part of it— notice and write about one discovery from your work in this chapter here:

IBL TOOLS & RESOURCES

- Self-assessment style: What is my baseline, What are my patterns, and, How does this serve me?

- Stages of Change (Prochaska & DiClemente)

- SMART Goals

- Breath work and Physiological Sigh

- Alignment of outside and inside

- Personal Stories:

  - Danna

  - My Feet

  - Lynne

Chapter Three

Emotional

Your willingness to feel will determine your layers of experience within yourself and those you care about.

THIS SECTION IS BUILT for you to jump right in using your Insight-Based Learning skills. You have been practicing self-assessment through awareness building, acceptance or not of elements in your TFBA and behavior, and self-determination for next steps. **This is the recipe for makin' lemonade.**

Take a moment and write down the **feelings you experience most frequently** and a related circumstance for each.

What themes emerged?

What stands out to you as you finish this first exercise?

Where do you **feel vulnerable** and uncomfortable?

Why is this so?

Being **truly honest** with yourself, how do you limit your experience of your feelings (limiting includes: avoid, deny, defend against, refuse to integrate)?

Using the awareness you just created, answer the next set of questions.

1. What would you say are the seven most common feelings expressed among people universally (across cultures, countries, etc.).

2. How hard was it to come up with seven?

3. Which feelings do you experience most (look at your own themes above).

As promised, here's the research-y information:

Social psychologist Paul Ekman is quoted in several works as having identified six or seven of the most common emotions universally experienced. In 2024 Ekman's work includes these six: **Happiness; Sadness; Anger; Fear; Surprise; and, Disgust.** Check out this website for in-depth descriptions and the most recent work by Ekman regarding facial expressions.

https://neurolaunch.com/paul-ekman-basic-emotions.

Social science researcher, author and acclaimed speaker Brené Brown has written in her 2021 book, *Atlas of the Heart: Mapping Meaningful Connection and the Language of Human Experience* that "...human emotions and experiences are layers of biology, biography, behavior and backstory." (Introduction p. xxix). She identified 87 separate feelings and multiple categories they fit in as a way to understand the range of emotions we experience.

Looking back on your responses, what do you see as patterns and categories — patterns are repeated thoughts, feelings and behavior. Categories are the types of thoughts, feelings and behavior. Here are two examples, feel free to define your own categories or use those in *Atlas of the Heart* for guidance.

- Category: Self-talk

- Thoughts, Feelings: I don't have the time to deal with all this, I am overwhelmed.

- Self-assessment/awareness: I think my time is too tight to attend to all the things I am involved in, I tell myself I am overwhelmed. I say I "am" rather than I feel overwhelmed and this makes me see myself as totally engulfed in the things I have committed to rather than examining my feeling of *overwhelmed*. Feelings are an experience, not my *being*. Feelings can be broken into manageable parts, overwhelmed is made up of xyz for me, I can take one at a time.

- Category: Avoiding conflict at work (could be creative tension, interpersonal conflict, authority interactions).

- Thoughts: They don't like me or my ideas, they don't even know me but they shut me out in meetings like I don't have enough to offer.

- Feelings: Excluded, invalidated, fearful of results to challenging perceived poor treatment, resentful, avoidant, anxious.

- Self-assessment/awareness: I am telling myself a story about whether they like me or not, I don't truly know if being liked is the issue. They have been a team for a long time, I am the newest person, I think I know how to present my ideas, but maybe not, maybe I'll observe others more. I still feel shut out, is it about me or them? I feel hurt, sad, confused and left out. I'm not sure what I can do about this. I need to find someone to check out my perception with, who feels safe for me?

You can see how our weave of TFBAB gets moving quickly to create misunderstandings and emotional stress. Creating your own method of self-assessment gives you an easily accessible space to **stop the swirl of thoughts and feelings** to check your own reality and find a place to **respond rather than react**.

Look at the defining elements in the Brown quote above, how do those fit for you? Take some time to examine this question to get the most out of your reflection.

In the first edition of *Lemonade* I included a list of 27 feelings with the simple opening, "Complete the sentence: I feel _____ when..." Included in that list were a few not on the most common lists by the researchers above, let's take a minute to add a few more feelings.

I feel **joy** when...

I feel **satisfied** when...

I feel **capable** when...

I feel **worthy** when...

I feel **understood** when...

I feel **validated** when...

I feel **empowered** when...

I feel **lucky** when...

I feel **self-conscious** when...

I feel **uneasy** when...

I feel **emotionally threatened** when...

I feel **out of control** when...

What patterns evolved when you added the list above to your list of feelings?

What are your thoughts and feelings about the possibility of so many feelings? In Brown's study she and her team found 150 feelings after surveying over 65,000 people and receiving over 500,000 comments. They narrowed the responses to **experiential categories**. Her work is seminal in the area of understanding the **weave of feelings and behavior,** I highly recommend *Atlas of the Heart* for deeper understanding as you engage in your own discovery.

You are likely experiencing a range of feelings as you work through these exercises. What is coming up for you?

Notice the increasing complexity in the list of 12, at **what point did you start adding thoughts to the feelings**? Your weave is part of you, what you do with it is up to you.

To put it directly, what feelings are triggered when you do feelings work?

What feelings are you **trying to avoid**, and why? (Yes, I asked a similar question earlier in this chapter, you are likely to see it again.)

Let's look at fear. Right in the eye.

What role does fear play in your life?

Look at your response, **what** situations did you describe? **Who** plays a role in your fear? **When** does fear creep up for you?

There are multiple books, podcasts, TED Talks and online resources on the topic of fear. I can't begin to cover the depth of them all in this workbook, however, you can look at **how much power you give** your fears and what your motivation might be for doing so.

Here's another feeling question— complete the sentence, I feel avoidant when:

Here's the power within your avoidant fear: **I am afraid I will** (state the behavior/feeling you are avoiding) **which means I am** (state the self-judgement you are making).

What have you discovered as the root of your active fear(s)?

Is this root fear something you have control over? Or, better and more realistically stated, is the outcome truly what you have control over?

Here's a truth I'm inviting you to wholly consider: We have influence over some things yet we **do not have control over** anything other than our thoughts, feelings, beliefs and attitude, and behavior (TFBAB).

Period. Sit with this for a while, make it a mantra if that will help keep this reality a focal point when you feel the desire to control.

Here's another internal quiz for you: What do you believe you control outside of your own TFBAB? What is your **factual** proof that you have this control?

If you answered the question above with an example, **are you sure** and what makes you certain you control these external things?

If you answered with an example to the above question, what is the **cost and/or benefit** of this control?

Lastly, what if you didn't really have control but influence, how would your example look different?

In her best-selling book *The Let Them Theory*, (2024) Mel Robbins offers clarifying reality statements about keeping ourselves focused on what we truly can control. She covers our relationship with ourselves and others in straightforward language. "*...let them* and *let me*. The more you allow people to live their lives, the better your life will get. The more control you give up, the more you gain." (p.45). Robbins' theory is in perfect alignment with what we have been working on in this section — how is your perception of your control over others and events **grounded in reality** and how is it impacting your daily living? Robbins suggests you let other live their lives and have their own perceptions just as you have yours. I highly recommend her book for further understanding in this area. She has a podcast and does speaking engagements   https://www.melrobbins.com/podcasts/episode-70

As a society we in the US are a very anxious group of people. According to studies, particularly after the COVID pandemic, US anxiety rates have risen considerably. The why of this issue is not a single event or situation, it is a mix of events, losses, self-efficacy beliefs, and externalization of locus of control. A study in 2020 at Penn State https://www.healthline.com/health-news/people-more-stressed-today-than-1990s revealed patterns in people increasing for age ranges in the 45-65 group who are juggling family, technology and life responsibilities.

Importantly, younger groups are reporting higher levels of anxiety, the American Psychological Association reports in 2023 twenty and thirty somethings are feeling overwhelmed with money stress in particular

https://www.apa.org/topics/stress/generation-z-millennials-young-adults-worries

Additionally, isolation is reported as a very real concern and issue for this age group. Interestingly, isolation has been an element of elder depression and a known entity for decades. Researchers are now finding ways to better define what is actually going on with people by using better descriptors and offering clearer definitions. This level of awareness is key in determining what is happening for you and how you can address it.

If you are feeling overwhelmed and you can't seem to manage those feelings right now, you have every right to use the emergency resources by calling 911 or 988 or your local mental health center for immediate assistance. A mental health emergency IS a medical emergency. Explain your condition if you make a call so that you can best be helped. If you feel that calling a friend, family member or if you have a therapist, and reaching out to them is what you need, DO contact them now. **You matter**.

Anxiety can feel like an energy with its own mind and presence, it can feel as though it chooses to ride along with avoidance quite comfortably and tends to fuel your fears. Describe where you feel anxiety in your body, where does it start and what do you fear will happen if it continues on its path?

Reflecting on all the writing you've done to this point, **where are you discovering** that your anxiety stems from?

What are you **willing to do** today about your anxious feelings?

You've done some deep digging regarding fear already. If you are feeling anxious as you go through these exercises take time to ground yourself and give yourself a break. There is no time limit for discovery, this is your journey, take small steps as needed. You'll learn about **growthful increments** in the next chapter that **clearly define small steps toward change.**

Try this quick grounding exercise:

- Sit or stand (as you are able) with your feet flat on the floor, feel your feet touch the floor, wiggle your toes, flex and unflex your feet working up to your ankles, calves all the way up to your torso—

- **breathe** in and **breathe** out at each transition from feet to ankles to calves to knees, etc.

- When you get to your torso, **breathe** in deeply and let it out for twice as long as you took in your **breath**.

- **Do this four times.** You can stop here if you feel a sense of relaxation, or, you can go full body in the same manner to get a deeper release.

- You can make up the path which arm is next, add a gentle wiggle, etc.

- **Just breathe** at every junction and end at the top of your head. Take the time you need to do this. Try it with music if you like.

- **Just breathe.**

Here's another **grounding exercise** I particularly love and do often, I learned this from my dentist before a root canal:

Get a lavender filled eye pillow or other size and type that is meant to be put in the microwave for up to 2 minutes to warm. Place that warm pillow on your abdomen just above your belly button and relax in a chair or on a couch, wherever your body is somewhat prone and your head is supported. Find your seated/prone spot, then notice your breathing and try to manage it as explained above. Try this for 15 minutes if possible. It's fine if you fall asleep, set a timer in advance.

If warm isn't your thing, try this: Using a cool cloth that is moist but not drippy, place the cloth over your eyes with a spot open for your nose so that breathing is not blocked. Do the breathing exercises above.

And yet another one: Using a face cooling mask try the same exercise. Or, if you like, put a cool cloth on the back of your neck. This relaxing technique has been recommended to relieve stress and migraines and can be done most anywhere in short, do-able time slots. Try these and find what works best for you.

If you are interested check out this site for 30 grounding techniques and information about why you might want to try them, **you are worth the time.** https://www.healthline.com/health/grounding-techniques.

This next exercise (*Lemonade*, p.120) is something I developed in the 1980's while working with families, kids in particular, when we needed to get to anger— what it was covering for and how it was being acted out.

What Is Under Your Anger Umbrella?

1. **On the umbrella** write the word Anger

2. **Beneath** the umbrella on the left side, write Fear

3. **Beneath** the umbrella on the right side, write Pain

Take some time to write the feelings that go with your fear and your pain. Write out the circumstances of each.

Here are some feelings often described in this exercise: shame; guilt; feeling left out; feeling "less than" others; awkwardness; lonely; too (fill in the blank); etc. What are you trying to cover with anger's primary expressions of fear and pain?

A really useful collection of feeling/emotion visual aids can be found at https://wholeheartedschoolcounseling.com/

where images include topics for adults and kids. I recommend you visit the site especially if you are having a hard time imagining **what else might be present** under your umbrella.

https://selpowerpack.com/wheel

Offers a set of stickers on a "coping wheel" for adults and kids. It's a little bit different than some items on the market and you might get some new ideas on coping strategies for a variety of emotional reactions in various situations.

Back to you with an important question—What are you **holding on** to most? What do you **fear letting go?**

There's lots of white space on this page, doodle, journal, express however you can your feelings related to your anger and the additional feelings you've discovered here.

What Else Is There?
List your feelings that live *within* Fear and Pain

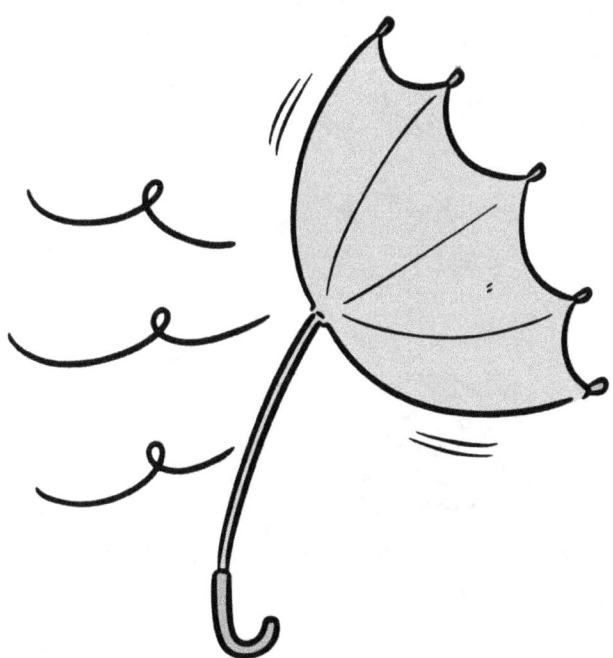

Sometimes people feel as though they can't express their own anger for fear of being out of control, perhaps fear of being inappropriate with words and behavior, and possibly fear of doing it "wrong" whatever wrong means in various families and relationships. Anger is a **valid emotion**, how you express it is completely up to you and you are **accountable** for your expression.

Some people, especially in relationships, try to get others to do their bidding by threatening anger or showing great displeasure and disgust. Have you had someone treat you poorly through their expression of anger?

Have you ever used your anger to manipulate someone or to get something you want — and specifically, if you KNEW that by showing your anger you would get acquiescence from another person?

These last two questions might carry intense emotional energy as you reflect on them. If so, do some journaling here, just free flow writing for seven minutes. Set a timer and allow yourself the freedom to express your feelings without a filter. Afterward, look for a pattern. Within that pattern is where your healing work can be found. Go.

Allow yourself to write freely…and do a little doodle here.

Another method to gain access to your thoughts and feelings, and to do some **self-soothing** is by coloring. Adult coloring books contain designs that are meant to help you change your focus by repetitive and intricate coloring (unlike children's coloring books) so that you can release the tension in your brain and body. If you prefer to use a children's book, go ahead, it's up to you, just give this proven method a try. I especially like mandala books and I have a huge box of colored pencils for my own practice. I think you'll be amazed at the difference coloring can make for you.

https://www.webmd.com/balance/features/benefits-coloring-adults

Several resources are available for anger work. *The Dance of Anger* written by Harriet Lerner covers relationship patterns with anger as the focal point and is an excellent place to start. Check out journaling workbooks and seek counseling if your anger is getting in your way of healthy living. As a matter of fact, if you do an internet search for anger workbooks you'll get a listing of the Top Ten Anger Books because there are so many. I came across the following site that has baseline anger management tools (note, there are resources for kids, teens, adults that will fit for developmental stages)

https://www.imhlk.com/wp-content/uploads/2018/02/Anger-Management-Workbook.pdf

Your body takes a hit from your anger, **particularly unresolved anger** that can lead to anxiety and depression. That's a big statement, and it's been known in medical circles for decades. It's up to you to decide what you are willing to do for your own health, for your life.

The Mayo Clinic's site has a wide range of articles, here's one regarding high blood pressure (anger elevates blood pressure).

https://www.mayoclinic.org/diseases-conditions/high-blood-pressure/in-depth/stress-and-high-blood-pressure/art-2004419.

In his groundbreaking book, *The Body Keeps the Score: Brain, Mind and Body in the Healing of Trauma* (2014) Bessel Van Der Kolk explores and illuminates how we hold our experiences **in our body** and the results of unexpressed trauma. He writes, "...the engines of posttraumatic reactions are located in the emotional brain." (p.206). He provides clear examples of situations that lead to physical symptoms and impact health within the whole body.

It's time for an important reminder: you feel your feelings and experience them, **you are not the feelings** — here's how to make a declarative statement: I feel really annoyed and it feels deep for me, anger is building within me, **versus**, I am angry.

Practice **I feel statements** with the types of anger you experience here.

In this chapter we have bumped up against trauma responses without specifically discussing and reflecting on them. I've added content on trauma later in this edition, please take your time getting there, try out the work that comes first.

Go back to the list of 12 "I feel x when..." sentences you completed. Select one that feels good, right on target, you know when you have this feeling, try to remember a time when you were dialed in to this feeling — what was happening and what role did you play in the experience?

What action are you willing to take today to have that same feeling?

How are you creating your own barrier to achieving this feeling? Or, if you don't think you have created a barrier in the present, how have you created one in the past and how did you work through it?

The sentence above is one of my *golden questions*. I use these to highlight strengths — *what do you have within you that you can access now for the results you want?*

Try this questioning on other feelings you've identified, see where you might go.

<u>Caryn's Story</u>

Caryn was adopted as an infant, she was raised with two siblings in a mid-size Minnesota town where being outdoors every season was simply the family culture. Caryn had a large extended family who visited often and participated in the family's version of broomball, badminton, forts in the woods and more. Caryn loved her family and all the activity, but she really didn't enjoy the bitter cold that came with some of the usual rituals. Caryn joked that her bio-blood must have come from a warmer climate and that her role was to introduce something that did not involve mittens to the family event calendar. Caryn made this proclamation early in junior high/middle school when she was finding her way into her own identity and empowerment. Caryn took on cooking as a way to be centrally included yet avoiding the ice and snow for an entire day. She asked for forts in the woods to include kayaking on the creek in warm weather and cooking out by the water with campfires.

Caryn described her family life as one of inclusion and that required self-efficacy if there was going to be change. She was rebuffed in the ways siblings go about things and encouraged by her adult family members to be creative. There were plenty of failed attempts at new games and some scary food concoctions. The keys to Caryn's success within her family were finding pathways through barriers, being creative, and being courageous to try new things that were as likely as not to be accepted by others.

If this sounds like a little bit too Minnesota nice, here are some other family dynamics: Caryn's adoptive mother was hit by a drunk driver when Caryn was ten. Caryn's older siblings were involved in school activities that kept them away from home so Caryn assumed care-taker tasks that were outside her 10 year old abilities and understanding. About a year after the accident Caryn's father and uncle clashed in a business deal they had been working on for several years, both families lost most of their savings and sense of security. It wasn't just financial security, but security in the sense that things will work out, that a temporary set back is temporary rather than a sentence to a life highlighted by loss. The family events got more physical between cousins, occasionally there was a broken nose or worse as tempers flared. Caryn was often torn between alliances but held firmly onto her belief that a family is an everchanging unit and with that come challenges to be managed. Caryn's brothers occasionally "counseled" Caryn on conflict resolution which typically leaned in their direction, but Caryn was a quick to understand the plot and learned the art of alternative action taking. While Caryn had a great many sources of input and attitudes, she attributes her worldview to her parents and particularly her mother.

The trait we see within Caryn is one of **resiliency.** Her early experiences created the emotional space, even though Caryn was quite young at the time, to take a pause, to look at the elements of the situation and create a plan.

In what ways have you developed **resiliency**?

When asked how people define resiliency they often say "the ability to bounce back." I am among the authors who describe resiliency as an awareness, set of skills and process that begins with both an innate and learned ability to see past the event and **seek a coping pathway.** The *verywellmind* website https://www.verywellmind.com/what-is-resilience-2795059 has some well stated descriptions and examples of resiliency.

Research with children in difficult home situations from the 1970's supported the nurture versus nature side of our understanding of resilience. They found that the presence of a person who believed in the child and supported them, sometimes with unconditional love, was key to the child developing the ability to cope with emotional challenges. Over the past ten years we've learned so much more about the nature side of resilience. Neuroscientists have studied a location in the brain where coping skills, through analytical processes and willingness to face challenges exists and can be observed when stimulated in clinical settings.

These two websites https://www.journals.uchicago.edu/doi/10.1086/69795and , https://pmc.ncbi.nlm.nih.gov/articles/PMC7215067/

contain studies written in clinical terms, if you love science you'll love these studies. If you like to bypass the clinical language and get to the behavioral or everyday language, then try

https://www.verywellmind.com/what-is-resilience-279505.

I like the *verywellmind* description because they discuss life areas and actions — take a look and when you come back to the question of "what ways have you developed resilience?" you will likely have a longer list.

Another easy to follow book has been written by Dr. Gail Gazelle whose work I discovered by listening to the Rob Orman podcast, Stimulus. Dr. Gazelle's book, *How to be Resilient: Simple Steps to Embrace a Positive Mindset and Build Inner Strength* (2025) will get you started on a clear path toward and into resilience practices.

Susan David writes in *Emotional Agility* (2016) that we have the ability to build skills and face challenges in our life areas that we may not have defined as options before. She takes the reader on a journey of reflecting at how we react and/or respond to situations and how we can create new to us responses. David uses the famous quote by Viktor Frankl, paraphrased here, that between stimulus and response we have the opportunity to pause, and in that pause, we have the choice to decide how we want to respond. This concept is probably one of the most important lessons we can learn, we DO have the choice in our reactions or responses.

Another **gem** from David is her description of being **"whelmed"** rather than overwhelmed (p.174). She discusses those times when we may be overcommitted and challenged to manage all the things we have going on — tasks, emotions, expectations of self and others, etc.

Laura van Dernoot Lipsky is the author of two important books on understanding and managing trauma. In 2009 her book (co-authored with Connie Burk) *Trauma Stewardship: An Everyday Guide for Caring for Self While Caring for Others* changed the face of what trauma looks like for those of us in the helping fields. Since then she wrote *The Age of Overwhelm: Strategies for the Long Haul* (2018) which provides readers with an excellent understanding of the process of being present, being mindful of our own decisions and ability to choose what we dive into and what we set aside. Her book has an extensive Notes section and bibliography.

> Here's a pro-tip for those of you who love to read and go deeper than the page you're on: **read what the authors you love to read, read.**
>
> Read the sentence above again. Here's how you find what writers read: I peruse footnotes, quotes, resources, bibliographies and any other citation an author uses when I want to find out how they learned about a topic. I mention books and articles a lot, I do that quite intentionally. Yes, this is the age of electronic information and generally whatever you find on the internet can be found somewhere in the ether, again. Things change. Resources like blogs and podcasts and websites open and close. I've linked several resources in this workbook that I find useful. Go to the places that you trust for accurate information and know, that while I am writing this workbook a year from now there will be even more resources that I could have cited. That's the beauty of being a life-long learner. **Keep searching,** it's a wonderful part of the journey for any life area.

One last concept and reference before we leave this section. Many of us grew up in families or situations that were dysfunctional to varying degrees. We might joke about it to keep the hurtful feelings at bey, but they are there as are self-doubt, judgment, perfectionism and a longing for "normal" whatever that is. One definitive and on target book about the dynamics of our own lives that are carved from the normlessness of our childhoods has been written by Lindsay Gibson titled, *Adult Children of Emotionally Immature Parents: How to Heal from Distant, Rejecting, or Self-Involved Parents* (2015).

I can very highly recommend this book, for every person I've recommend it to the content has been like opening a door and more than one have said it created an "awakening." That's strong evidence that a book explains the subject authentically. If you choose to read Gibson's book, take it in bits and pause where you need to, you are on your own discovery pathway and you may need some space to digest the information then plan your response. It might be a good idea to do this reading with self-care items nearby, i.e. your glass of water and being in a comfortable space.

IBL TOOLS & RESOURCES

- Emotion Definitions

- Anger Umbrella

- Looking Deeper and "Behind" Anger

- Discovering Anxiety

- Discovering Resiliency and Wellness Practices

- Personal Stories:

    ◦ Caryn

Chapter Four

Intellectual

Wellp, here's a big topic.

THIS CHAPTER IS ABOUT information processing, not intelligence. It's about how and why we use what we have, and how we can grow more branches to access more information with which to make choiceful decisions. It's also about making connections with others and how our connections impact thought processes, learning, values, decisions, and worldview.

In recent years the terms **intentional, mindful, and purposeful** have been used nearly everywhere to describe the process of assessing our own awareness and to give meaning to an experience. We label TFBAs as individual elements and in clusters that make up an experience. We take in information through our senses and categorize it. We use our imagination and curiosity to seek adventures and form memories. We seek understanding by comparing new information to that which we've already cataloged. This life area is fascinating and invigorating, here we go...

I'd like to start us off with a song, check out Aretha Franklin's *Think* and perhaps pay a visit to this website to learn a fitting interpretation of the song. I personally just love to dance around and sing loudly and joyfully with it. https://melodyinsight.com/aretha-franklin-think-lyrics-meaning/

How do you feel after listening to an inspirational song? Or reading something that really resonates with you? Or possibly hearing an amazing speaker, or even engaging in movement that provides the endorphin release you were looking for? Take a few minutes to imagine each one of these things and feeeeeeeel the feeling. What are you experiencing? Make a few notes here:

There is **no way to unweave the thread** of our intellectual life area from all the others. It's you **engaging with yourself** and noticing who you are.

I'm a big fan of quotable quotes, especially when they convey concisely what I'm attempting to describe.

> Albert Einstein said, "Imagination is more important than knowledge, for while knowledge defines everything we know and understand, imagination points to all we might yet discover and create."

> Here's another favorite, "If you believe you can, you probably can. If you believe you won't, you most assuredly won't. Belief is the ignition switch that gets you off the launching pad."
> —Denis Waitley

I started this chapter in *Lemonade* with: "I will not succumb to self-oppression." That's pretty heady stuff. And yes, this chapter is about that, yet so much more. And another thing, over these twenty five years I have made a very conscious decision to state **what I WILL do** rather than what I won't. It turns out our brains discount "I won't" statements. **Our brains hear the intention** in what we state we will do which fires up our action-taking neurons.

Human development theories have existed for millennia, debate exists over when our personalities form, the role of nature versus nurture and so on. Science over the past two decades has offered an explanation regarding adult-ish brain development to occur around age 26. Again, -ish.

https://stories.uq.edu.au/the-brain/2022/timeline-of-brain-development/index.html

Here's a very scientific article on how adult neurons form and regenerate https://pmc.ncbi.nlm.nih.gov/articles/PMC4026979/

Now, given all of that here's the bottom line: we are amazing humans with the capacity to learn and change. There are several personality development theories and far too many citations to include here. You've likely heard of Freud, Maslow, Piaget, Erikson, Adler, Skinner, and Perls whom I mentioned in the Introduction. As decades and even centuries tick by studies on human behavior, motivation and personality continue to develop. Patterns prevail and that's where the focus is for your work. Let's take it down a level to **traits and preferences** that create your outward self.

There seem to be five general (as in very generally defined) personality traits that we exhibit and that can be tied to thousands of thoughts and behaviors, the acronym is OCEAN:

https://www.berkeleywellbeing.com/big-five-personality-traits.html

Be careful NOT TO READ JUDGMENT into the labels.

1. Openness — creative, curious

2. Conscientiousness — thoughtful, helpful

3. Extraversion — sociable, outgoing

4. Agreeableness — kind, empathic

5. Neuroticism — sad, anxious

Traits are measured on a ***how much of this is present and how is it exhibited*** scale. As you look at the Big Five list take a breath and ask yourself how much you show of these traits on a daily basis. Or perhaps at work versus home versus with friends/family. **Traits are dynamic**. Our personalities are not static and we are not stuck one way or another. **We have the gift of choice.**

Trait indicator tools focus on **preferences** on how we learn, communicate, and show feelings. Our preferences influence our decisions. General patterns are consistent, yet may be different in settings i.e. work relationships versus home life. You might have fun doing the short quizzes in a magazine or perhaps engaging in tools like *Real Colors* or the *Meyers Briggs Type Indicator*, there's also a book and survey by Dr. Gary Chapman that is currently popular titled *The Five Love Languages: How to Receive and Express Love*

https://www.simplypsychology.org/five-love-languages.html

If you search for love languages you'll see models of five, seven, ten... All these models and theories make it clear we are **curious beings and we are trying to understand** ourselves by building guideposts and pathways. If this kind of research or assessment piques your interest there are professionals who provide services for assessment and interpretation of the results.

Cultures like school or work create *codes,* everyone inside knows what you're talking about but outsiders might not. How we attribute meaning is one level, followed by our value of the labeled thing, followed by our willingness to commit or fight for this labeled thing. We shift our understanding and willingness to ascribe to labels as we mature. Labels without meaning are not useful.

Try this: In five to seven words, describe yourself—

How did **you choose** to use your words? A sentence, or perhaps a bullet list of descriptors or traits? Perhaps something others have noticed and told you?

I asked a client to describe herself a few years ago. She drew a tree with multiple branches and leaves, the roots were intertwined and extended past the canopy of the tree. On each root, branch and leaf were descriptions and events. I was amazed at the amount of effort she put into the exercise and I felt truly honored that she shared this level of awareness with me. Feel free to express yourself with a drawing. Go with your style, that's the message here.

Take a look again, what really fits, what would you like to refine, what is aspirational in all reality?

Circle three strengths and reflect on those, own your strengths and think for a minute about how those strengths reflect your values and your actions.

The next link is an excellent resource to the origins of the term **information processing** and how it is a metaphor for our brains being like computers that was first coined in the 1950's. Yep, rock and roll, Elvis, and information processing models became part of the social and academic fabric in the 50's.

https://www.thoughtco.com/information-processing-theory-definition-and-examples-4797966

Further, a well written review of the models that brings us up to date on the research can be found at https://psychology.iresearchnet.com/developmental-psychology/cognitive-development/information-processing-theory.

It's time for a confession. I am an information geek. I LOVE this stuff. For me, this is FUN. And it's okay if you're not an information geek, **just be you** and **seek what interests you.** Maybe make a list about things that you're curious about, **seek out something new today**.

I realized last night that I haven't included movies or TV shows as a form of information resources. If you are a movie or TV fan, you probably realized that in the last chapter where I failed to mention movies like *Inside Out* (2015) with a sequel released in 2024. My oversight is a perfect example of how we go to our preferences first, then look at larger pools of information. Like concentric circles the further out we look the more we take in. All kinds of art and performances, sports, nature, academic pursuits, self-care practices, meditation, and on and on provide input for us to process. **What we pay attention to gets remembered.**

I visited Ireland in 1992 with a general plan, a large backpack and my camera. Back then film was the only option, keep that in mind as I tell you the next part. I hiked every day. I visited pubs, I met all kinds of people from all kinds of places. I even met a couple from Iowa who wanted to take my picture because I was a "local girl near the bookstore" and before I could really launch into how I was from the mid-west and I thought they were asking where my family was from in Killarney, I was in their photo memories. One day I was hiking in a park and I decided to sit on an ancient wall and use only my senses rather than my camera to create my memory of the place. I could wax poetic about the sun and butterflies and the color of the wildflowers, and yes, I saw all those things, yet what I recall is an experience, not a photo. I very intentionally sat there for perhaps thirty minutes and took in the feel of the place, the sights, sounds, the wind in my hair and I sat quietly while

all of those things happened naturally around me. I have some lovely photos from the trip, too, but that day stands out in my memory as one of the definitive experiences of that trip.

Fast forward to today. Actually yesterday. I read a wellness practice that suggested we do exactly what I described above, **to be present in the moment** and allow that experience to define that moment. Allow input and the knowledge that becomes clear in that moment. Break down the larger experience into **meaningful parts**. Give it a try and see what comes up for you. Neuroscientists tell us that when we relive these moments we further cement the memory and release the neurotransmitters that relate to a feeling of well-being.

Scientists also tell us that our strongest sense is olfactory, our sense of smell. Our recognition of a smell is the fastest message to our brain that triggers a memory. Here are some favorites people mention: freshly baked bread/cookies, their pets, the lingering scent of cologne. Flowers and plant matter have a wide range of olfactory stimulation and for some people who have allergies, the mention of the smell can send them into a sneezing fit. Powerful stuff. Make a note or two about a smell you **particularly enjoy** and let the fondness of the memory wash over you.

On a personal note, I've kept one of my mother's purses. My mom loved to shop for shoes and purses. She had something of a reputation among her friends and coworkers as it related to her collection. She loved to find an outfit to go with her shoes. As for her purses/handbags, large and with pockets were the two rules. She'd do a fun springtime outing to find something under $30 as a kind of sales rack treasure hunt. The purse I kept still has her scent, it's kind of a mix of her perfume and the leather from her wallet. When I pull out her purse and look through it all those scents seem to rise up and for a moment it's as if we are talking about going on a shoes and purse shopping adventure.

We're going to shift gears a bit into values, decision-making and worldview.

When you looked at the OCEAN list what values popped up for you? You would know they popped up because you would have had an emotional and intellectual reaction to the words. For instance, do you value the idea of being an extravert and what that might look like for you in your behavior? Or, possibly, did you have a reaction of "oh, I am more introverted, are they saying that's not good?" See what I mean here? What did **you question** about yourself with OCEAN?

Have you ever done a values sort exercise? You'd recall it if you have in the last five years or so, you can do it electronically or with paper cards/checklists. There are usually about 100 values and you are asked to select the ones most important to you, perhaps 10 out of 100. Let's do a shorter version here, please complete this list—

My 10 most important values are:

It's often difficult to come up with a top 10 right off the bat. What did you discover?

If you want a bit of assistance in finding words, try

https://drjudyho.com/wp-content/uploads/stop-self-sabotage_Values_Card_Sort.pdf

You likely noticed that Dr. Ho's weblink has the name of her book included, I haven't read her book, but the **card sort** is what you'll find across social science fields in the public domain. It doesn't hurt to consider how you might engage in self-sabotage of your values or goals... just sayin'.

Decision-making models show us **thinking pathways** common to types of decisions. Most cognitive-based decision models use a timeline, personal values, motivation, reward/punishment ratio and desired outcome matrix.

Let's **break that down to a flow** and you can fill in how you make decisions (primary style, not impulse or under the influence, etc.)

1. **When** is important to the whole picture — is this a quick decision or one where you can give it time? What do you prefer?

2. **What values** are related to the topic/decision? How important are these values and this decision (not important, somewhat, very, or extremely important)

Note: who else is involved in this decision? Add that to your values statement. How important is this person/people?

3. **Why** are you making this decision?

4. What **could go** wrong, what **could go** right?

5. What are you **hoping** to have/experience/gain/avoid by this decision?

Now, look at your answers, how many **micro-decisions** came into play as you worked down the list?

Which area has the most micro-decisions?

What action, if any, do you think you need to take based on this exercise?

Compare your thoughts to your feelings regarding this decision. Are they aligned? Which is the **stronger pull** for you, thoughts or feelings?

What you've been practicing is called **incremental analysis**. It's a great skill to have for any kind of decision.

Have you ever heard the term being an "incrementalist"? I first learned the theory as it relates to government and here's a link that will give you more than you asked for in regard to incrementalism. https://www.encyclopedia.com/social-sciences/applied-and-social-sciences-magazines/incrementalism

---

For the purpose of personal **growth**, here's the short version as I've defined it, let's call call it **Growthful Increments**:

- **Take small steps.**

- **Assess your experience.**

- **Define progress.**

- **Determine next steps.**

- **Be willing to amend your plan.**

- **Embrace adaptability.**

- **Celebrate your successes.**

- **Allow "fails" to be successes that need reworking.**

- **Repeat**

This bulleted list is exactly what **IBL asks you to embrace.** I stated in the Introduction that the model is easy to understand, yet the **work takes intention**. In order to create intention you have to **understand the increments**. Take time to make your own meaning of each step in the process.

Here's another pro-tip for change: The more you do something, the more it becomes habit. One of my favorite books on this topic is *Atomic Habits: An Easy and Proven Way to Build Good Habits and Break Bad Ones* by James Clear (2018).

I quite literally have to control my urge to quote Clear over and over in this section. On Page 39 Clear uses a great question to start the reader's thinking: "Who is the type of person who could get the outcome I want?" WOW, what an excellent inquiry for reflection — this goes back to our conversation earlier in this chapter about labels, who are you? How do you operate in your world? What do you want and how do you want to obtain it?

Clear's *Four Laws of Behavior Change* may resonate deeply with you, I highly recommend you read his work and sign up for his emails, here's the website for his app

https://atoms.jamesclear.com/

And now for worldview. Yes, that IS a big topic. As I thought about addressing it here my first impulse was to say: Specific or General? I recognize this is not a commonly asked question on a daily basis. The following link is one of the best explanations I've seen

https://www.masterclass.com/articles/what-is-a-worldview

So, that's where you might start. What is your **overall worldview** and how have you **built it**?

Notice the word "built" in the previous sentence. Worldview is learned first from our family or those who raised us early on, then refined by our own perceptions, later amended by the values we choose, lived in a manner that aligns with the elements that have built it to a certain point, and refined again through deeper understanding that comes from experience. After reading this process, **add or clarify your definition** of your worldview.

As you can see, this last area if inquiry is a nice way to **gather all the things** we've been talking about in this section **and weave** inextricably with all the others.

Gather your thoughts here on the exercises in this section, what stood out for you?   Where do you plan to take action?

What's one idea or thing you want to take from this section and **share** with someone?

IBL TOOLS & RESOURCES

- Personality Traits OCEAN

- Values and Decision-making

- Pathway Toward Change (© 2025)

- **Growthful Increments (bolded because it's a big deal)**

- Worldview

- Your Weave

- Personal Stories:

    ○ Keri

Chapter Five

Social and Relational

In the sweetness of friendship, let there be laughter and the sharing of pleasures. For in the dew of little things, the heart finds its morning and is refreshed -- Khalil Gibran

It's early morning on January 1st, 2025 as I write this chapter. My phone is buzzing with texts from friends and family. I feel the essence of the Khalil Gibran quote as I read and respond to each person. For me, this an experience of my heart being full. I feel grateful.

I am also very aware that for some of us this can be a lonely time. Most of us have or have had a gap where we'd like deeper, more rewarding relationships. In this chapter we're going to move quickly into connection, belonging, accountability to ourselves and others, and, nurturing relationships that we value. We'll look at boundaries and conflict, fear, loss, and, our depletion and renewal cycles.

We are to varying degrees social beings. Connection is clearly related to health and well-being. https://hsph.harvard.edu/news/the-importance-of-connections-ways-to-live-a-longer-healthier-life/

Finish this sentence, I am connected to others by:

I have a **connection gap**, it's due to:

What did you discover above about your **value of connection**?

In recent years researchers have been focusing on the experience of belonging. It's a powerful thing to feel as though you belong. And we know when we don't feel as though we belong. Write about your own feeling of belonging, what you experience and if you invite others to belong with you.

Time for definitions. Social, in the context of IBL refers to non-relatives, i.e. acquaintances, friends, workmates, teammates, peers, schoolmates, etc. Relational refers to family, **however you define family**, blood relative or not.

The rationale for the differentiation between social and relational is that communication, expectations, motivation and willingness to maintain relationships differ. Personal history differs significantly and as we know, nature and nurture play roles in connection.

The desire to be *seen and heard* has been written about in recent years. The desire isn't new but the clarifying description resonates with most everyone. Elements of what I call *humanship* provide the foundation: active listening; curiosity with kindness; respectful inquiry; informed support; and, invitations for inclusion that meet the person's interests and abilities.
Describe your practice of *humanship* here:

Revisit your answers above, using the social and relational definitions, **add more** to your response.
What did you discover or at least **own** in terms of the status of relationships?
What appeared in your work that reminded you to **reach out** to someone?

Here's a link to Robert Fulghum's bestselling book that keeps it simple and it will likely make you smile.
https://www.penguinrandomhouse.com/books/56955/all-i-really-need-to-know-i-learned-in-kindergarten-by-robert-fulghum/

Try this exercise:

Using the target start with yourself in the middle, then work outward first with your closest relationships, out to various types of connections that you define, i.e. partner/spouse, immediate family by name, friends, acquaintances, workmates, teammates, etc. Feel free to make big circles and circles inside of circles, whatever fits best for your **understanding of your flow of connection** with others. It might help to identify activities you engage in with certain people to get a better understanding of where they fit in your circles. You can indicate exits, too, if you had a relationship with someone and they have moved/been moved to a different spot.

You can see the **dynamics in action** with this exercise.

How many levels did you define?

Where do most of your people fit?

One key ingredient in feeling connected is **psychological safety**. Here's a useful link to understand the broader aspects https://en.wikipedia.org/wiki/Psychological_safety

It's said that that psychological safety is the most studied dynamic in workplaces and leadership. Coined by Carl Rogers in the 1950's the focus at that time was space with others where someone could feel safe to be creative and trust that their ideas would not be met with heavy criticism and invalidation. The meaning has grown to include trust and connection as we think of it now with regard to communication dynamics, respect, inclusion and support. Currently psychological safety has become an element of workplace well-being assessment — we'll get into that in Chapter Seven.

Take a look at your circles, where does psychological safety come in? Go a level deeper with the idea of safety, indicate where you feel **emotionally safe** and **physically safe**.

Write here about your findings.

Because we all live within the scope of our TFBAs we have endless emotional experiences with others. The next block centers on how you experience conflict.

Create your own definition of relationship conflict (any kind, romantic, work, friends, family, etc.)

Perhaps a continuum would help as you ponder this question. On one end start with 0 or no conflict, on the other, 10 or high conflict. BTW, it's normal to have disagreements in values, ideas, preferences — a life without conflict would be a life without connection.

0 ——————————————————————————————————10

Make your own hashmarks where you feel you have conflict and label them with a person and/or situation.

Where do you have conflict and what is **your honest role i**n the conflict?

You are likely struggling a bit here with the types of conflict you experience and how they impact you. Again, because this is a **dynamic** between people it evolves. Here's a link to learn more about types of conflict. https://www.healthline.com/health/interpersonal-conflict

After considering types of conflict, i.e. factual, opinion, values, policy, etc. where do you find yourself **having the most conflict**?

What might you be **doing to start or maintain** conflict?

How many "I don't" or "they do" statements did you make? What is your honest role in these situations?

What is happening within you that this kind of conflict takes place (wants, needs, fears, goals, past trauma)? Take time to analyze each of the conflicts you listed on the continuum. What pattern do you see? List those conflicts and patterns here so you can see them.

List your conflict management skills, what is **your go-to**?

If you listed a current conflict, what action can you take and by when?

Define your goal: I am (going to + action) _____ because I want _____.

Remember SMART goals we discussed in Chapter One, you can apply that outline here to get more specific. I've found that when people are uncomfortable, and conflict tends to make them feel uncomfortable, they avoid being specific and avoid clear time frames for action. Check your plan, is it SMART?

After addressing your selected conflict, come back to this page and describe what you did, how it went and how you feel. By the way, feelings are experiences, they are not US. That is, **we have feelings but we are not the feeling.** Check your writing style, if you've written "I am...." change it to "I feel...".

Gina's Story

Gina was hired into an existing workgroup of 15 staffers at an established firm. She had previously led a team of six before taking this job, she was prepared to be "one of the team" rather than in a position of authority and felt invigorated by this change. Gina's supervisor described the team as a family and frequently mentioned that everyone was expected to look out for each other. Gina wasn't sure of the definition of "looking out for each other" yet assumed she'd know the type of situation when it arose. Gina's co-project manager told her that their supervisor was skilled at looking out for himself when once again, he mentioned they needed to have each other's best interests in mind should a complaint come along. Gina decided to stand back a little and observe the interactions between as many people as possible without seeming unfriendly or distant. She wanted to have a sense of dynamics and boundaries before making herself vulnerable.

Gina's work was complimented by her teammates and she felt things were going well with them yet she had a gut feeling about her supervisor that she couldn't shake or identify. Her teammates often went to happy hour and invited Gina who typically declined. Gina felt she was socially different from her teammates and tended toward organized events that were either sports related or had a cultural element like an art exhibit. Gina simply didn't like the bar scene. Gina was able to form cross-unit friendships that evolved from shared projects, she and the two people on those projects had dinner from time to time. Gina's supervisor told her she was not making enough of an effort to be friends with her own teammates, her "work family" as he put it and while he put it in terms of a suggestion his directive was clear, she was to attend the next happy hour invitation.

Gina's sense of boundaries and respect was being battered, she felt as though she was being forced to spend social time, non-paid time with people she liked just fine as workmates but had no interest in as friends. She felt like she didn't belong, suddenly, and according to her supervisor, her teammates felt that she was being standoffish and rude by declining their invitation. Gina felt the invitations were just a symbolic offer and not authentic since none of the teammates had ever engaged her in deeper conversation than project specifics at work. Gina attended the next happy hour. Some of the spouses and friends of her teammates were also there so the gathering took on a bigger event feel than just a few work people getting together. Gina was still in her first six months of her job, she knew a little about some of the people there and tried to get to know the "extra" attendees. She mentioned sports and local events, she looked at pictures of pets and kids. She also kept an eye on her watch because she was determined to make it for 90 minutes and then politely leave. That would be enough, right?

The supervisor popped into Gina's office later that week to check on her experience at happy hour. He said he knew she'd gone as he asked a couple of team members about it. He himself did not go because "As your leader it would not be appropriate to be out in a bar." The mixed messages seemed to keep building with this supervisor, what did he expect of her? Gina took the opportunity to tell her supervisor that he had hit on something there, that she prefers other activities rather than going to bars and that she has met her teammates for happy hour, was glad she did, yet for the future she planned to go the gym and a class at a local college after work most nights. In her mind she was setting a boundary and stating she would not be available to go out with co-workers.

Gina's supervisor reacted with a terse voice and stated she needed to be friends with her teammates so that they would respect her. He could see she was friends with two people on different floors of the building and she needed to try harder or she'd never be respected by them.

Gina journaled all of this when she went home and tried to decipher the dynamic that was going on. This all felt very dysfunctional to her and that she was being disrespected by her supervisor rather than her co-workers. It was confusing and disturbing to feel personally attacked for her value of her personal time. Gina told herself she'd give it 90 more days and re-examine her feelings and experiences. She thought about confiding in the teammate who had made the comment about their supervisor, but that didn't feel quite right. She was on new hire probation for her first 6 months, after those passed, according to the personnel rules she could go to a higher manager with her concerns. But how did she define them? For now she'd journal and try to gain clarity.

What are your feelings as you read Gina's story? What did you identify as potential issues in varied relationships? What would you advise Gina to do and why?

Here's a topic just gaining more open conversation in general: Communication styles with behavioral patterns based on **trauma responses** and, or, **neurodivergent** processing.

What does this mean? I cannot do these two topics justice here so I am going to share a few behavioral patterns known in the literature and recent research. As you've come to expect, there are links for more information and I highly encourage you to seek understanding of your own or someone you know who's behavior might be part of a condition that is more about neurological architecture than choice.

There's a label called Adverse Childhood Experiences (ACEs) that has been used for three decades or so. Children who have experienced abuse and/or lived in situations where their safety was threatened and who suffered harm often have different brain development than those who did not experience those conditions. The kind of harm, the amount of harm and the duration on all figure into the neurologic impact. The presence of abuse does not mean that this always happens, yet it has been found frequently enough to be able to define patterns of academic, social, and emotional development issues. Of importance, I must mention that **threats and abuse as adults also causes neurological change**. Here are some websites for more information:

https://institute.crisisprevention.com/Trauma-Informed-Care.html/?utm_source=bing&utm_medium=cpc&utm_campaign=gen-tofu-search&msclkid=db7dc35876a819cd6d6ca4f70b9219c6

https://pmc.ncbi.nlm.nih.gov/articles/PMC6428430/

https://neurolaunch.com/how-does-childhood-trauma-affect-the-brain/

Here's a short quote from the website Neuroscience News: *"By leveraging AI to analyze brain scans, the research highlights how early abuse rewires pathways associated with emotions, empathy, and bodily understanding, potentially leading to difficulties in learning and decision-making."*

The websites listed here go into various levels of scientific findings and perusing them for understanding is enlightening. Just coming to an understanding that **empathy is highly effected** by an abuse history, not only on the psychological and communication level, but on a **structural and executive functioning** level is necessary when considering why you or someone you have a connection with struggles with empathic expression.

https://neurosciencenews.com/brain-development-child-trauma-22558/

Some behavioral patterns that are often trauma related include but are not limited to:

1. Hypervigilance — staying attuned to perceived threat after a threat situation has passed or is possible but not active in the here and now

2. Hyperarousal to stimuli — seemingly overreacting to sounds, smells, touch, visual cues that are known or unknown triggers of fear

3. Social withdrawal — triggered by an event or anxiety, the person withdraws from relationships

4. Anxiety and panic attacks — related to PTSD(S) can be triggered by a wide variety of stimuli

5. Episodic intense expression of anger or other feelings of loss of control with limited ability to describe the feeling fully

6. Change in focus or productivity at work or school — can be sudden or gradual, often related to PTSD(S) triggers and depression

7. Boundary issues being too porous or too rigid.

Very recent research has revealed much more insight into the information processing and resultant behavior of people with **neurodivergent brain** functioning.

What is neurodivergence? The term itself is not a medical diagnosis, it is a description of a wide set of patterns that may or may not have a medical connection. It's a way of making sense of information and viewing input that is different than people considered neurotypical (NT). Here are some resources:

https://my.clevelandclinic.org/health/symptoms/23154-neurodivergent

https://resilientmindcounseling.com/neurodivergent-examples/

Note: I have not worked with this provider, I included their website because of their easy to understand definitions.

The book by Rudy Simone, *Aspergirls: Empowering Females with Asperger Syndrome* (2010) does a great job at explaining how females with AS (Note: the term Asperger Syndrome/AS is no longer used, Autism Spectrum Disorder/ASD is the preferred terminology since 2013) view their world, how they make decisions and communicate, and how they function and struggle in relationships, school, jobs, social activities and mental health concerns. One very important point is this: people on any spectrum are just that, on a **spectrum** of behavior, feelings, experiences, knowledge, and functioning. Always be careful about trying to **diagnose** a pattern, be aware of the elements of a pattern and what works, what doesn't and why. One common trait for people with ASD is that they very frequently feel misunderstood and believe it is their fault which triggers guilt and shame. Many people report that their neurodivergence is just part of who they are, it's not a problem to be solved or changed, but understood by those willing to see them for who they are.

Ethan and Ellen's Story

Ethan and Ellen are siblings who grew up outside of New York City. Both are gifted academically and both seem to be "behind" socially, all the way into and after college. Ethan works as an architect and loves the quiet of his job, the opportunity for productivity and creativity instill a great sense of satisfaction for him. He has one friend from work who he "games" with for hours after work and with whom he has attended a gamer convention recently. Ellen is finishing college this year, she is in her sixth year of a typical five year program and has struggled maintaining focus to make it to graduation. Ellen is working part-time to have spending money, the work is repetitive which has its own energy of being soothing at first and boring after a couple of hours. Ellen is making herself keep this job though she feels kind of numb after her shift, in the past when she has gotten bored she quit. There's a long list of past part-time jobs. Socially Ellen has acquaintances but no one she'd really call a close friend. Ellen has a history of "flying off the handle" or seemingly overreacting to perceived slights by others and tends to burn bridges.

Ethan and Ellen's parents have difficulty understanding their children's choice to be rather solitary and they worry about Ellen's mismatch between her intellectual ability and her lack of focus. Neither Ethan or Ellen had any special education or social skills referrals, both easily completed the gifted programming at school and reportedly felt no anxious feelings about college. Ethan didn't "walk" at graduation though he was in the top 2% of his class and had academic awards that would be presented to him on stage. He doesn't like crowds and didn't want to bother with all the attention and closed in spaces. His parents were disappointed about graduation but let it drop after more than one heated exchange on their part. Ethan tends to shut down when things get conflictual often to the point of never resolving the conflict and carrying a grudge over long periods of time. Ellen is already feeling anxious about graduation, she wants it to just happen and not have to plan for it. She could graduate this semester if she completed a project that is several months overdue. She feels a bit out of control of her life and with no set direction. She has migraines and doesn't exercise like she used to. Her parents ask often what she is going to do with her degree and where she plans to live next. Ellen has no concrete answers for them and feels defeated. Both Ethan and Ellen say that they understand each other better than anyone else and they hold this connection dear. They have shared childhood secrets typical for siblings to keep, and when there has been something significantly hurtful they've only told each other. They text on a weekly basis and see each other at their parent's house on holidays. They both state that the holiday visits are for their parents, that they care about them and want to make them happy, but they also feel constricted by social expectations.

From your own perspective, what do you think is happening in the lives of the siblings?

From what you have experienced in your own life, what similarities are there?

What seems "normal" and what seems "atypical" in terms of development and behavior?

There is **no right answer** here, it could be a bunch of different things or a singular condition. Without more detail we don't know how either feels or sees the world or what they want past what has been articulated in their story. This is a good example of how we all "have a thing" regarding our behavior or outlook, our social skills can ebb and flow as we try new things and meet new people, and we can be smart and still not in the zone of getting things done. The reason for sharing this story is that is shows a variety of behavior that also has similarities to, but are not necessarily diagnostic of any mental health or information processing condition. Both could probably find value in upping their social and coping skills, yet, are they motivated to do so?

Take a moment to ask yourself this: How did you use your own experiential lens to understand the elements of Ethan and Ellen's story and their personalities?

Did you picture a town outside of New York City you might be familiar with?

Did you create a mental picture of Ethan and Ellen? Their job sites and activities?

Picturing people and parts of stories is what we do to understand them. We use our own lens and that's where things can get tricky. You might know a lot more about towns around NYC than I do so your picture of Ethan and Ellen's hometown might be quite different from mine. This is my point, we project our knowledge and experience onto the canvas of a story and we might not have all the information necessary to create a complete picture and accurate understanding.

Take a minute and ask yourself:

- Did I project something into Ethan and Ellen's story that was not shared in the elements of the story?   If so, what?

- Is my projection something I have experienced and might need to look at more deeply?

- Are there actions I'd like to take?

Also, keep in mind the story shared with you is Ethan and Ellen's, it might have many similarities to your own and you might be feeling triggered right now based on the details of their story and any projection you may have done. Take a minute to assess your feelings related specifically to this story and your **reactions.** Write your reactions here:

And now, let's move to the skill of **creating a response**. Rather than react to the stimuli of the story and your feelings, what would a healthy coping response be? Write about that here...

You've worked through several scenarios in this section. You may have related to some of the stories and it's possible some boundary issues of the past or present have been triggered. Take a few minutes to **pause** here and **go back up through the paragraphs of this section**, fill in missing information. Notice any lingering feelings or thoughts. **Make notes here:**

Let's take a breath, truly, take a deep breath here because this is deep work.

If you identified a conflict where your physical safety is at risk please take time to contact a service provider for resources and guidance. The number for the National Domestic Violence Hotline is 1-800-799-SAFE (7233). If you are in immediate danger call 911 or if you are at risk of harming yourself, please call 988 or 911. **You matter.**

Emotional abuse is a real thing, again, you can use the domestic violence number listed above for resources. Interpersonal violence happens on a continuum, you can get help before you get hit. https://www.thehotline.org/

Boundaries are key to every relationship. Nedra Glover Tawwab wrote *Set Boundaries Find Peace* (2021) and created a workbook to go with it. I highly recommend this book for everyone, actually, but especially if you are wondering if you need to tune up your boundary setting. My good friend Michelle with whom I worked for several years and who's knowledge I deeply respect states frequently, "Boundaries are life." It seems we pay too little attention to boundaries and are then left wondering how someone crossed ours so easily or why someone else's are so rigid. Tawwab explains three types of boundaries in her book (healthy, rigid, porous) and gives clear examples. This link to a TherapistAid worksheet gives a nice outline to get started.

https://www.csueastbay.edu/shcs/files/docs/hf---types-of-interpersonal-boundaries.pdf

Let's take a look at how you learned what boundaries are and how to set them. The **short definition of interpersonal boundaries** is how you allow people to treat you, i.e. how they speak and act toward you, how you say no to someone, and how you allow yourself to be vulnerable with someone and allow them to know you.

Go back to the exercise where you created your circles of connection and relationships. **Describe how you set boundaries** with at least three people using the short definition above.

What would you like to do differently?

Here's something to think about: who in your life seems to have **healthy boundaries**? Why do you think their boundaries are healthy? What examples can you give that include statements and behavior that they have that **you'd like to try**?

What if you asked them how they set boundaries?

Diving into the depth of boundaries is outside the scope of this chapter, which is yet another reason to check out the resources I've listed, however, just considering your patterns with people in your life gives you a good awareness of how you may or may not be setting healthy boundaries for yourself. **Only you can set your boundaries.**

Because we value something we also fear losing that something. Setting boundaries can cause loss within a relationship. This is often the reason people don't set a clear boundary or stick to one, fearing the loss feels greater than the perceived gain by setting a boundary. The truth is two-fold: You deserve to have healthy boundaries, and, your fear is generally greater than the loss itself. Relief is on the other side of the boundary. Your walk **through the muck** has to be done to get there.

Let's wrap up the boundary conversation with this question: **How would you like to feel after setting a boundary** with someone?

And, what will it take to start setting that boundary, perhaps today?

In a relatable flow of thought, the book *Establishing Boundaries with Kids: A Parent's Guide to Negotiating Limits and Improving Parent-Child Interactions* (2022) by Kristi Miller offers practical options for boundary setting. The author uses a clear **Try This model to help parents** understand why a technique might work and what they might be facing as barriers to success.

Within the last decade a communication method has emerged that I can best identify as **"saying the awkward thing out loud."** I absolutely love how this has evolved and it seems to be generational, so thank you Gen whichever because you have opened up a door that is often left banging shut and no one quite knows what went wrong and how it went so badly. Let's discuss.

Cultures vary in how people share thoughts and feelings, we get that, yet there seems to be a universal experience of feeling awkward and not wanting to seem awkward, yet, there's no right or skillful way to get to the thing that is creating the awkward issue without being, well, awkward. So nowadays some **difficult conversations** are being started with simply naming the awkward experience that is about to take place and blazing a trail right into the content. That's **courage**! The sentence usually starts out something like, "This might seem awkward to discuss, I know I feel kind of awkward, but..." How and when have you used this conversation tool?

How do you say the awkward thing? Or, are you still avoiding it? This little gem is a great way to open up authentically to another person and validate their awkward feelings, as well. Give it a whirl, refine it to fit your style, I think you'll be glad you did. I know I feel relief when I use it, **rather than dancing around** a topic, I express that I am not sure of the best way to discuss the topic and I feel awkward. Usually a shared feeling is experienced, clear understanding comes of it and often, laughter.

Here's a concept that is often felt yet not described clearly. We have **natural renewal and depletion cycles**. Renewal or fueling is when we take in or allow ourselves to receive good energy from others like nurturance, genuine compliments, feelings of belonging, and connection. Depletion is when we give and give and give without the balance of renewal. Fueling and depletion happen around most life areas, and particularly within relationships. Describe how you refuel and how you know you are entering depletion.

In 2023 I created a model to describe in depth the layers of the renewal and depletion cycle. For our purposes here, think of yourself as a vessel, your **body holds all of your life areas** in one wonderful container that can always be added to as learning and fulfilling experiences happen. This container can also be **incrementally drained** by the outgo of emotions, intellectual endeavor, physical activity, illness, reactions to boundary crossing, real and perceived threat, significant loss, and truly, the aggregating effect of any combination of these and other life events. In a sense, this is a definition of life. All life areas have an ebb and flow to them, however, in the case of unbalanced renewal and depletion, renewal doesn't keep up with the depleting factors. Of note, balance is how you define it, it's not a 50/50 ratio, but what balance or internal harmony feels like for you.

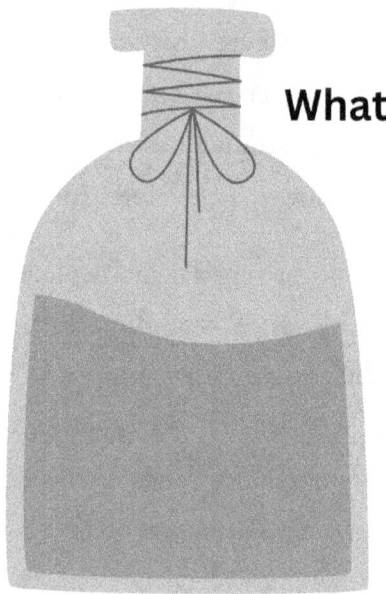

What goes in, what goes out?

List as many renewal factors you can think of — things that bring you joy, happiness, contentment, curiosity, fun, etc. This is your list, define it as best fits for you.

Next, list as many depletion factors that you can think of — things like deadlines, feeling overwhelmed, conflict, money concerns, health issues, etc. Again, define these as best fits you.

What does your cycle look like, when does it happen and with whom or what setting?

What role do boundaries play in this cycle?

What is one thing you can do right now to refuel? Try not to put it off, doing something for yourself in the here and now is a choice and a gift. You matter.

When you read that last question and sentence, what was your reaction?   Why so?

The next layer in **understanding the status or health of your renewal and depletion cycle** is to assign numbers to determine way points, like on a measuring cup. The reason for this is simple, it helps to know when you are getting low and what you need to do to refuel. In my own visualization I have hash marks at the side and each has a numeric value, I check myself daily by asking Where am I today and what is happening that I feel I'm at this number? What do I need to do to maintain or refuel?

Go up to the example and define your waypoints, give yourself a rating for today and ask yourself if this is something you want to maintain or adjust today. Then make a plan. Remember the **Discovery Pathway?** This is assess and act…

This short section is about big topic: How you value your time and energy is how you **value your well-being**.

Describe your relationship with yourself, your inner relationship.

Look back through this workbook, you've done a lot of writing and reflecting so far. What have you discovered about your **relationship with yourself** in the previous life areas?

Physical:

Emotional:

Intellectual:

What patterns do you see within these areas that are part of your **well-being weave**? Be sure to write about the healthy things, not just the areas for refinement.

Recall that in the first chapter I asked you to say kind things to yourself and use the **"is it true, is it kind"** test to shore up your self-talk. Apply that here, as well.

As this chapter comes to a close here's a quote Joseph Nguyen cites in his book, *Don't Believe Everything You Think: Why Your Thinking is the Beginning & End of Suffering* (2022, p.33) "If the only thing people learned was not to be afraid of their experience, that alone would change the world." — Sydney Banks

IBL TOOLS & RESOURCES

- Connection and Belonging
- Practicing Humanship
- Social/Relational Circles
- Psychological Safety
- Conflict Types and Awareness Building
- Boundary Types and Practices
- Awkward As Authentic Communication
- **Renewal and Depletion Cycles (FitzPatrick, 2023)**

- Personal Stories:
  - David and Cheri
  - Gina
  - Ethan and Ellen

Chapter Six

Spiritual

Seeking meaning in something greater than ourselves takes many forms.

OVER THE YEARS I'VE looked at my own definition of spirituality and that of researchers and authors. We're all on the same page regarding the kind of connectedness to something greater than ourselves philosophy. This online article from the University of Minnesota does a nice job outlining types of spirituality and the difference between religion and spirituality https://www.takingcharge.csh.umn.edu/what-spirituality

What part of your life's journey would you describe as spiritual?

How has spirituality helped you with situations and decision-making?

During what kind of circumstances do you turn to your spiritual beliefs/practices for clarity?

Bob's Story (Lemonade, 1999)

Bob is a spiritual person who has been diagnosed with an always fatal disease. When he was first diagnosed he was given about a year to live. At that time no one that Bob's doctor was aware of had made it past several months.

Bob came to work and told us about his diagnosis and the prognosis. He stated he was going to make some major life changes and they would start immediately. Bob began very consciously planning for his life, not his death.

He got his legal affairs together, he moved to part-time work, he began traditional chemotherapy for his illness and he made another significant decision about his healthcare: he added Eastern medicine that included acupressure, acupuncture and what we'd call mindfulness exercises today, all of which were monitored and supported by his physician. Bob was invited to a sweat lodge in the traditional Native American manner and regarded the experience as profound. Bob was approved for medical trials and experimental drugs. During this time of seeking intervention, Bob moved to a small town to be closer to a group of people he considered like-minded spiritually and in daily practices including farm-to-table diet, yoga, regular meditation, and tons of outdoor activities.

Bob's health continued to improve and he moved out of state. He volunteered for a support group dealing with the same illness he had and in a year's time was working as a community advocate, liaison and public speaker on the medical condition and its effects for patients and their significant others. According to Bob his remission was due in very large part to his spirituality and worldview that included so many others outside of his immediate concerns. He had purpose and purposeful work.

Bob's spiritual practices included geographic places where he could go to meditate, hike, camp, and take others to share the experience with. He made it a habit to visualize these places when he couldn't get there. On a snowshoe hike with Bob he told me his change in diet, activity, stress and his deepening spiritual connection had the most impact on his survival.

When Lemonade was published in 1999 Bob had undergone two surgeries and his condition worsened. He had been living what he called his best life for five years after his diagnosis. Bob passed away from his illness. At his memorial many of us shared how changed we were by knowing Bob and having walked alongside him especially the past five plus years. Bob was a connector of the best sort and he made a point of connecting with others to learn of their journey, hopes, and challenges.

As you read Bob's story what resonated for you?

Perhaps you yourself have been struggling with a medical or other condition that has left you spiritually parched.

List your **spiritual strengths and struggles**.

> And, so, now what? Where will you take action today?
> https://www.verywellmind.com/how-spirituality-can-benefit-mental-and-physical-health-3144807
> One element of spirituality is feeling nurtured, that you have a space and in that space you are safe, you belong, you can grow. The space can be geographic like a hiking trail, or it can be in your mind's eye, or better yet, both. Write about your space. Draw an image that represents your spiritual space.
>
> Another element is the sense of flow and of awe. I've mentioned this before, positive psychology offers several exercises. I like the writing of Mihaly Csikszentmihalyi https://positivepsychology.com/mihaly-csikszentmihalyi-father-of-flow/and the definition he offers of the flow state. Another online resource is https://www.flowresearchcollective.com/blog/what-is-flow-state

Religion, as we know is different from spirituality, however, one engages in some or all of their spiritual practices within the structure of religion. Write about your religious beliefs and practices.

What would you like more of in your spiritual life?

Where will you go, who will you contact by when to meet your want?

Looking at your own sense of your spirituality, what is the **difference between your wants and your needs**?

As you look at the notes you've made throughout this workbook, how have your insights **linked spirituality** to your other life areas?

IBL TOOLS & RESOURCES

- Discovering and Defining Your Spirituality

- Wants versus Needs

- Spirituality Within Other life Areas

- Personal Stories:

    - Bob

Chapter Seven

Educational and Occupational

The only place success comes before work is in the dictionary -- Vince Lombardi

ALBERT EINSTEIN IS QUOTED in educational materials as having said, "I have no special talent, I am only passionately curious." And this, in my opinion, is truly the essence of learning.

People seeking knowledge and understanding are using their curiosity to continue learning. **Seeking** is the key, seeking to apply new information to previously learned content and seeking to create new types of action based on learning. Again, this is a great definition of Insight-Based Learning.

Academic achievement is only part of education. Ask yourself what kind of **knowledge, skills and attitudes** you gained in school. Make some notes here about school, starting at any point that you think has been or is currently **significant**.

Describe **your value of** academic engagement, i.e. formal schooling K-12; college; trade school; certifications; etc.

What level of education have you accomplished? about your education?

What are your thoughts and feelings

What would you like to change about your educational level? What about ongoing learning in your life?

What will it take to make these changes and what is one step you are **willing to take today**?

Colleges and universities have job service offices where you can take assessments and receive guidance on steps toward specified jobs. College academic and career counselors are great resources, you don't have to be a student to contact a college to see if they have available services. There may be a fee, yet **if you are curious** it's worth the money. There may be grants to seek information in your area, again, contacting your local trade school or community college could be a great step.

If you enjoy **self-directed learning** you could check out master classes online at https://www.masterclass.comMany types of classes are offered through Master Class, they utilize "bite size" learning models so your time is not impacted like a traditional online or in-person class.

Some book clubs take an academic approach to reading and if this sounds like fun, check out community or your library's clubs/reading groups.

TEDx and TED Talks (TED stands for Technology, Entertainment, Design) offer in-person events all over the country and in Canada, worldwide speakers are represented on endless topics and the forum is a fabulous launch pad for professionals who are gifted speakers and communicators. https://www.ted.com/talks

I am a huge proponent of **continuing education after a person gets into their job.** Some professions require a certain amount of training/education hours per year. This kind of learning is an investment in yourself and growing your future. When you can choose which classes to take, choose those that are **meaningful to you**, not just checking a box.

Jot some notes here what your field or future field requires in terms of educational background, knowledge, experience and, skills—and how you will get those in place.

How much continuing education do you engage in now and how do you access it?

What are you willing to pay for or access yourself as an **investment in yourself?**

Scottie's Story

Working as a grocery checker in a large national chain store did not sound like much of a career when Scottie was going to college. She studied business and psychology and thought she'd somehow combine the two when she graduated. Getting a college degree was THE ticket to the American Dream, Scottie had been told that repeatedly and right up to graduation day. That was eight years and two kids ago. Scottie married her high school sweetheart after coming back to her hometown following a stint in Chicago looking for the right job. No job seemed right for Scottie. She wanted to be with people, not in an office at a desk. She wanted to do something with variety and that kept her moving. Scottie tried working as an administrative assistant at a mental health center after being told she could work her way into an internship with some of the counselors there. The internship did not materialize, Scottie felt betrayed and disappointed. She moved on to medical transcription for several months, her knowledge about healthcare helped with the vocabulary and she was more skilled at transcription than she thought she would be. Still, she felt unsettled, not happy or purposeful with her work. She moved home.

Scottie and Steve got reacquainted and were married — the wedding was a big social gathering of old friends and extended family. One of Steve's uncles worked as a general manager at the large grocery store in town and mentioned to Scottie's mother that Scottie would be an excellent customer service cashier because she was so clearly detail oriented and outgoing. Scottie started out as a checker and realized she was having fun connecting with all the neighbors and local patrons. She moved up the ranks at the store and as time went on she was promoted into front office positions where she was well respected for her work ethic, knowledge of the industry and ability to coach new hires to develop interpersonal as well as task-related skills.

Scottie joked about using her degree to be a grocery checker, yet, she came to embrace the career she was forging and found a pathway to engage her interests in human development and communication with business process. Scottie discovered she valued the stability of the job at the store, the pay range was better than she had guessed before being in the field, and she had what she considered excellent health benefits. Scottie held a professional position as was her goal, and she found purpose in her work.

I'm inviting you on a little side trip into a discussion of the difference between **time and task management**. It took me a few starts to decide where this topic fits, and as you can see, we are here. I am often asked how to help people with time management and my answer is this: you can't effectively manage time without understanding what the task will require. One of the biggest complaints in work settings is that there is not enough time to get the work done. Let's take a minute to break a task down and experiment with what is required:

Task: Adding data to a pre-made spreadsheet that will require adding another column to be accurate.

Assess:

1. Do you know what this spreadsheet program is and have you used it before?

2. Do you understand how the data is to be entered and by when?

3. Do you know how to add a column to an existing form and potentially how to recognize if the form is "locked" in its formatting?

4. Do you know who to go to for help with any of the above?

If you answered no or not much to the first question your time on task is going to be a lot longer than someone who is proficient at spreadsheets. This is how overwhelm creeps into our worklife without much warning. The same exact thing can happen with any academic or learning task, if we don't have that learning anchor or previously learned and retrievable information we easily spiral into burning precious time to get the task done. So, breathe — and let's look at options.

1. What have you learned so far in this book about breaking things into doable parts?

2. What do you know to do from past experience when you need more information to move forward?

3. Who and what resources can you access for help on this ?

Obviously if you have to learn something new your task is going to take longer than something you accomplish every day. Here's where the discussion of efficient versus effective enters in. You can have one without the other, and while it's a nice goal to have both, it's not always best or even a good practice. Think about times in your life when this might be true, write about where efficiency was in place but lacked effectiveness, i.e. got it done in a timely manner but the resulting product wasn't all that great and perhaps had to be redone.

Write about a time when you created something effectively and the efficient use of time became a burden to move too quickly which resulted in conflict with deadlines but a good product was produced.

> You see where we are heading here. Until you have an understanding of how much energy, learning, and supporting tasks go into a seemingly single task you can't manage the time for completing it.

Write about an instance where you have figured out the layers of a task, the time it takes to accomplish them and how you feel about the results.

Describe some of your **best time/task management skills or habits.** Here's an example from my work life: I use those wonderful little colorful notes that can be affixed to things. I like to make one for my day and check off the to-do items as I go. Often supporting items have to be added as I discover more layers to a task and I look at my daily calendar to decide where I'm going to fit that in. My co-workers joke with me frequently about my notes, they work for me and give me the visual cue I need to keep moving on my tasks.

Your turn:

There are myriad helpful tools out there in bookstores and on the internet as this is a very common issue. Finding your style is key for your success. Here are some links representing multiple styles and advice.

https://www.dalecarnegie.com/en/time-management-goal-setting?

https://www.udemy.com/course/8-effective-time-management-tips

https://extension.uga.edu/publications/detail.html?number=C1042

Maslow knew that people deeply desire purposeful work. Defining your work is a place to start. If you participate in volunteer work, include that here.

What do you engage in that you consider your job or work?

Describe the purpose you feel in your work.

What might be missing for you in your work as it relates to purpose?

So now you have potentially identified a gap between what you have and what you'd like, perhaps even something you might need. How will you integrate this purposeful element into your work?

Maybe a special project? What would that look like? Jot some notes here:

Perhaps training in a specific area (tasks, leadership, certification).

In each previous chapter you've done **gap analysis** just like this one, you know what to do next in terms of action planning, what are your next steps?

My next steps are (do what by when):

Statistics in 1999 stated about 60% of workers were happy with their workplace. Workplace engagement includes much more than happiness, however, it's an important ingredient in keeping people employed and avoiding turnover. In 2019, before the pandemic, statistics were somewhat the same, people were needing more but not sure how to get to a fulfilling status. Engagement studies started appearing in all kinds of work settings.

Surveys like Strengthsfinder 2.0 https://www.gallup.com/cliftonstrengths/en/strengthsfinder.aspx have become very popular.

Gallup, an internationally known and much used resource in employment trends provides current insight about what workers say they want and need as of 2023 going into 2024 at

https://www.gallup.com/workplace/547283/workplace-trends-leaders-watch-2024.aspx

Executive coach and speaker Dr. Rob Orman collaborates with physicians and other professionals in his podcast **Stimulus** about work related concerns, not just those of medical professionals, but for anyone who works at something. He brings in knowledge and guest speakers from a wide variety of life skills practices and can be found online at https://roborman.com/category/stimulus/.

Another set of key workplace concepts is that of attending to people as people and their collective vision of their work including where they work. Chapman and White (2011, 2012) wrote *The 5 Languages of Appreciation in the Workplace.* Another important area is psychological safety, I've mentioned it before, yet finding it in the workplace makes a world of difference. Amy Edmondson is largely responsible for what we currently understand as Psychological Safety. Her work is based on decades of research and her model clarifies four essential areas where Psychological Safety can be practiced and refined. You can access her site at https://amycedmondson.com/psychological-safety/.

I especially like and use her book: *The Fearless Organization: Creating Psychological Safety in the Workplace for Learning, Innovation and Growth* (2018). Additionally, here's a link to LeaderFactor, the company started by Timothy Clark who wrote *The Four Stages of Psychological Safety* (2021).   https://www.leaderfactor.com/

> We all take on roles that come naturally, like being supportive or helping find information, providing guidance, being a wing-person, etc. Think about what you are doing now in any of these roles, **what brings you happiness or satisfaction?** What would you like more or less of?

Have you considered **yourself a leader**, if so, how so? if not, why not?

It's useful for everyone to consider **leading from where you are.** Today. What are your skills as a leader, how do you lead quietly and/or how do you provide leadership and support to others around you at home, at school, at work, on teams or clubs? Make notes below:

Links that may be of interest:

https://www.shrm.org/topics-tools/news/how-to-lead

https://www.linkedin.com/pulse/why-leading-from-where-you-so-important-your-career-shanna-a-hocking/

https://er.educause.edu/blogs/2018/12/more-than-a-title-lead-from-where-you-are

And here's a book I'd like to recommend: *Leading From Where You Are: How Every Person Can Help or Hinder the Collaborative Culture* (Greg Robinson, 2017).

In my current position I have the honor of working with personnel statewide on wellness practices and building a culture of well-being. This work is a labor of love for me. In some ways my professional journey has been similar to Scottie's in that I had a vision when I started out and I ended up through a variety of unforeseen employment opportunities in a task area I've wanted for decades. My title doesn't describe my work well. My work is much broader than the division where I work — that's kind of the beauty of being in a space that can be expanded according to identified needs, collective curiosity, and support of people in leadership with titles that clearly emphasize positional authority. I have purpose, meaning and the ability to grow in my work and workplace. I feel lucky, fulfilled, excited and focused most of the time. Sometimes I also feel exhausted. That's a harmonious dance for me.

IBL TOOLS & RESOURCES

- Self-directed Learning
- Gap Analysis
- Time and Task Management
- Values Alignment
- Pathway Building

- Discovering Leading from Where You Are

- Personal Story:

    ◦ Scottie

Chapter Eight

Financial and Legal

It's up to you how complicated you make these areas -- your actions are quite tangible in the past, present, and planning for your future.

Let's start with a very important question: What is your **relationship with money**?

The way to **pull apart the threads here is to look at your spending habits**, where do you spend money? Why do you spend it there? Where do you think you need more money? How will you access the money you think you need? And lastly, how much debt to earning and savings do you maintain? Write a few sentences on these questions.

What **patterns** do you see?

"The only way you will every permanently take control of your financial life is to dig deep and fix the root problem." — Suze Orman

Suze Orman is a financial advisor on the national stage, this quote really defines the area for your discovery.

What is one root problem, if any exist, to your earning or spending habits?

What **feelings are connected** to this root problem?

What **"should"** statements do you make to yourself about your spending or saving?

What **barrier is in place to keep you from behaving** the way your should statements suggest you would benefit from?

> And so, now what?
>
> If nothing changes, nothing changes. What is something you can honestly say **you want to change AND are willing** to take the necessary steps?
>
> Try small, incremental steps first. What are they?

Forbes is quite well known for its list of wealthy people and successful businesses. Here are some financial success tips that might be useful as good, common sense https://www.forbes.com/sites/financialfinesse/2023/02/27/how-to-set-yourself-up-for-financial-success.

Mike's Story

In a conversation I had with Mike he stated he had never thought of the idea that a person has a relationship with money. Money is a thing in his mind. It's a way to get something you want or to help other people. As he heard himself start to define money he then heard the attributes he associates with money — it has value past the monetary. Mike's husband thinks he overspends on trivial things. Mike thinks it's fun to pick up an item here and there for amusement. Mike's husband has re-homed several of these items and Mike has either not noticed or not said anything. Mike buys something online almost everyday. They give their delivery person a holiday tip because they have gotten to know them from daily visits.

Mike buys quality clothing from name brand stores and he loves to shop for his husband. They are foodies and enjoy outings to boutique stores, they both believe in a good haircut. Their disposable income covers the way that they spend their money, though, they both value savings and retirement planning for a time way down the line. They donate time and money to charities and often take their nieces out to cultural events. Vegas calls to them on occasion.

Mike buys things secretly. Not gifts or something planned, but something impulsively from the gas station convenience store. He has lanyards and sunglasses and more gum than he can ever chew. This behavior is the thing that got Mike's attention on his spending. He saw his credit card bill and felt panicked that he'd have to hide it from his husband because he didn't have a logical explanation for the purchases. He just likes to purchase.

As you read Mike's story, what do you think his relationship with money is?

If we remove money from this story, what is the focus?

And now let's take a look at **legal matters** in your life. Again, it is generally up to you how complicated you make this area. We'll look at situations and then, behavior that maybe or has caused you some trouble.

Most of us come across a situation in our lives where legal advice or at least knowing our **rights and responsibilities** impacts us. Make a list below of those times, for you, so far, i.e. inheriting money or objects, being called to jury duty, getting a speeding ticket or being in an accident, being named as a power of attorney for someone's medical issues or death, small claims court action, business start up/closing, divorce — to name some common reasons you might have legal involvement.

For each item on your list write your **current status**, short-term action needed on your part, and plan to resolve the issue.

> If you have several situations pending it could feel *whelming* as we discussed in Chapter Two, maybe even overwhelming. Break each item into doable action steps with dates for the steps. This way you are setting clear goals for situations that could have several layers.
>
> How many of your **legal situations identified so far are inter-related**?
>
> Of those that are inter-related, where can you get the **most benefit by resolving one** of the issues? Describe why this area seems most beneficial and how it impacts the others.

And, as you would likely have guessed, how does your legal issue(s) effect your financial life and the other life areas in general?

Shifting from what might be external events of which you have or had no control over, what legal situations are you involved in now that have been of your making or choice?

Again, this could include some of the examples above, go ahead and make note of those with a star that shows your own actions and accountability.

What about criminal charges? Have you had charges placed against you that you are dealing with now or in the past? Include multiple speeding or other traffic tickets that have a pattern, include DUI/DWAI even if there is just one — what are the consequences of your behavior?

Going deeper, are there other criminal charges where you have court appearances and have used or have need of an attorney?

What happened?

What outcome do you want and why?

What **level of honesty** are you being with yourself about this situation?

If none of these situations fit at all and you have no legal encumbrance, then you have little to work on here. Take a moment to write about legal problems that you **dealt with** before they became a legal problem (if any exist).

Finally, what is your view on legal issues overall and how do you live your values?

If you need an attorney you can start with this government website https://www.usa.gov/legal-aid Another way people often find attorneys is by word of mouth from friends and family. An internet search will bring up tons of listings.

IBL TOOLS & RESOURCES

- Dynamics of a Relationship with Money

- Personal Accountability Elements
- Complicating Our Lives
- Finding Resources
- Personal Story:
  - Mike

Chapter Nine

Volitional

Embodied strength starts with embodied awareness. -- Pamela Meyer, Staying in the Game

THE UPDATES IN THIS section are significant, I have very intentionally set out to live my life noticing my own acts of volition and define them in categories more descriptive than accountability or decision-making or binary options. In *Lemonade* I wrote, "Choiceful living is propelled by volition" (p.115) and I believe that today. What I've learned more about is the deeper levels of **how this is true** and *what volition in action looks like* from a place of intention and mindful practice.

I've asked you on page after page to look into yourself and ask sometimes challenging and fear-inducing questions. I've said over the years and in *Lemonade*, your fear is typically worse than the event — to refine that a bit, your fear of the results of your actions or an event is typically worse than the thing you fear. Not always, there is no always, for the most part, yet, finding courage within to keep moving **through your fear is your key to living a life of volition**.

In her book, *Real Self-Care (Crystals, Cleanses, and Bubble Baths Not Included)* (2023) Pooja Lakshmin describes The Four Principles of Real Self-Care (p.xxiv, Introduction) as:

1. Set boundaries with others.

2. Change how you talk to yourself.

3. Bring in what matters most to you.

4. This is power—use it for good.

As I mentioned in the introduction to this book, there are several models, most are simple yet not easy. Reflect for a moment here on how you might be practicing Lakshmin's Four Principles.

Go back to the last reflection and insert the words **I choose to... notice within yourself, your thoughts and feelings, how adding your words about choice may have shifted your experience of your sentence.**

Lakshmin also says that real self-care is not a noun, that it is a **verb.** That's exactly the essence of *Lemonade*, then and now.

Author, executive coach and host of the Abundantly Clear podcast, Malorie Nicole writes in *The Abundance Decision: The Intersection of a Thriving Business and Fulfilling Life* (2024) that we need to practice "radical honesty" in a way that serves us best as we look at our patterns and decide "...who you want to be in the world." (p.61). Again, this is a great definition of how to be intentional, mindful and truly choiceful.

In recent years articles have been posted about how many decisions a person makes per day, perhaps you've seen some of these. Here's a link that gives an overview of decision-making categories by type of need: https://www.pbsnc.org/blogs/science/how-many-decisions-do-we-make-in-one-day/

Depending on who you read, you can generally say we make many more decisions per day than we actually pay attention to. Perhaps 35,000 decisions in one day. And according to one article, each of those decisions is re-made one or two times per decision. Literally and figuratively **mind-boggling**. It's no wonder we get spun up in our own anxious thoughts and fearful non-starts. Dan Harris, in his book *10% Happier: How I Tamed the Voice in My Head, Reduced Stress Without Losing My Edge, And Found Self-Help That Actually Works — A True Story* (2014 and 2024) uses the term "monkey mind" that he learned from a meditation master to describe all that spinning and bobbling and getting no where or even backwards. *Monkey mind* is considered a function of being stuck in an ego-centric emotional and intellectual churn (p.89). Harris also hosts a podcast by the shortened title, 10% Happier, where he describes life decisions and the role of meditation in taking a break to step back from the **chaos we are imagining** and look at the event in workable, realistic pieces.

By now you have likely developed a pretty good level of awareness about your own thought and feeling patterns, how you use them to make clear-headed decisions or use them to avoid the list of TFBABs. In what way do you create monkey mind for yourself and in what conditions?

What's it **doing for** you?

I especially like a statement on Page 103 of 10% Happier where Harris writes, "Mindfulness represented an alternative to living reactively."

And so, what is **living reactively doing for** you?

This is where we do a gap analysis: **In which circumstances do you live responsively and in which do you live reactively?** Take time to write clear details.

I, like other authors tend to frequently reference a quote by Viktor Frankl about the space between stimulus and response giving us the opportunity to consider our actions. As it turns out there are several writers that may have actually made this now famous statement in various forms but none who have published the exact quote as it's attributed to Frankl https://quoteinvestigator.com/2018/02/18/response/. What's clear is that it is a worthy practice to think before we act. Ah, sounds so easy.

I have a dear friend who describes herself as "an emotional animal" with a chuckle, yet, she means it. She has **big feelings felt deeply**, and she tends to respond from a feeling place, she senses the proverbial saber-tooth tiger ready to pounce before she gets to potential analytical options. She gets there, of course, and she's adept at finding solutions to tiger things, yet she has to consciously rework her initial reaction into a rational response and override her initial emotional alarm (a brain structure called the "amygdala" signals the alarm). We all have our styles, others are more driven by thought processes and are able to step past the threat or pain signal to see a situation as **elements** of the saber-tooth tiger as opposed to a roaring giant cat. The great majority of us use a combination of these brain signals to find a harmonious mix for a functional response. Recognizing what works, what to refine and what to let go of is how we live an **emotionally agile** life.

My friend says she is a feeler. I describe myself as a thinker. Neither of us is all or nothing, we have preferred styles of being in the world. These styles relate directly to our sense of self and as author, educator and ski racer Pamela Meyer states in *Staying in the Game: Leading and Learning with Agility for a Dynamic Future* (2023) we create our own **meaningful identities** (p.82). In short, what this means is that we select TFBABs that we accept as defining who we are and how we relate to others.

> Describe the meaningful elements of your identity — you've had a lot of practice in this workbook excavating your TFBABs, take a moment or 7 minutes with a timer, to free-flow write about your own **meaningful identity.**
>
> Here's a tool, **do a scribble here**, you know, like in grade school where you make free handed looping lines to color in and thus create art work. Neuroscientists have found that reflecting on your thoughts as you scribble or doodle **opens up pathways** and connections for you to access your inner workings. Try it here:

Reflect on your writing, does this fit your perception of yourself? Add more, refine, it's yours, do with it what you like to make it most **meaningful,** today. Not aspirational as in "someday I'll..." but today, write more about your identity and what you appreciate about yourself.

Write about how you move about in your world, **how you engage intentionally** in a meaningful way.

In Chapter Five you took time to map relationships, you answered questions about how you interact with others and how you invite them into your personal space. Belonging and being **part of** are crucial to good health. Meaningful identity in this sense includes how you carry and share your worldview, how you express yourself and what you are doing to learn more about others.

Author, and founder of Breaking Glass Forums, Cynthia Owyoung quotes Verna Myers, VP of inclusion strategy at Netflix as having said, "Diversity is being invited to the party. Inclusion is being asked to dance." *All Are Welcome: How to Build a Real Workplace Culture of Inclusion That Delivers Results* (2022, p. 5).

How choiceful are you in **your outreach** to those who are not like you?

How often do you **feel included?**

What would you like to do differently in the area of diversity, equity, inclusion and belonging in your own **personal** space?

I've included the DEIB content to purposely move your thinking to a broader scope. You might feel uncomfortable with the notion of very intentionally going out to learn more about others and how to do that. I heartily recommend Owyoung's book as a place to start. We grow when we get out of our comfy space.

Describe how you **look outside of your comfort zone** to learn new things. Perhaps doing the exercises in this book could be a good example?

When I strike out on a new adventure I often use my mantra of "Strength. Wisdom. Courage." as a starting place. Depending on the circumstances I visualize success as I understand it in the present and set intentions to experience a successful try at the new thing.

Take a few moments here to write your behavioral steps toward a new experience, describe your purpose for it, your intentional thoughts and play it in your mind's eye as you practice success with this new thing. Refine as needed to make it fit for you.

If you need to go out and learn something before you can do your new thing, go learn it! Then, try on the practice again. Keep at it. You are creating your **choiceful living pathway.**

IBL TOOLS & RESOURCES

- Defining Volition

- Understanding Your Decision-making Process and Preferences

- Weaving Feelings and Thoughts

- Getting Uncomfy

- Choiceful Learning for Choiceful Living

Chapter Ten

Go.Be.Do.

Every day holds opportunity.

THIS IS THE CHAPTER where much of **the weave comes together** in practice. You have been peeling apart layers of threads to understand your thoughts, feelings beliefs and attitudes that lead to your behavior, your reactions and responses.

In the early 2000's I created a wellness presentation for probation officers and community partners called **Go.Be.Do.** Since then I've used this mantra as a call to action for seeking experiences, creating memories and living a life of well-being. You can rearrange the words to fit your flow, that's the beauty of a mantra, it's yours. Here are some action items to get started.

Go to a physical place where you feel content, give yourself time to let the feelings sink in, hold on to the visual picture, the sounds, and any other senses that you notice. Stay there as long as you like, and importantly, **create a mental memory** to bring back that feeling so you can access it in your mind's eye for future visits.

Choose two more feelings, perhaps excitement, curiosity, awe, belonging, kinship, etc., two feelings that are of high value to you, and do the same exercise you did with contentment. You are creating a mental storehouse of well-being practices for the times when you need a little pick-me-up.

Note: when you describe your visualization and your feelings your brain releases the feel good chemicals just as if you were there and these feeling tend to last for hours, **especially when you describe them to someone else.**

For more information on the "molecules of emotion" as they are described by researchers in a 2024 emotional neuroscience article go to https://neurolaunch.com/chemicals-in-the-brain-that-cause-emotions

MBTW's Story

I have a wonderful friend, MBTW who does quite a lot of volunteering for animal and people causes. One night a few weeks ago she called me, she had just been volunteering to provide food and clothing for a local shelter and outreach program. She'd been there for hours and while she was physically tired she was jazzed with the feelings of purpose and connection. I felt her energy and we talked for a while about the things we've shared in the 20+ years we've known each other, and also about how we value being of service to others. I was jazzed after our phone call.

*There's just one short story and illustration of sharing our energy and fueling others. I hope you'll consider a **Go** that provides shared energy on a regular basis.*

> **Be** who you are and who you are becoming. Notice what feels solidly YOU and what is evolving that you are learning to embrace. Write a few lines here about yourself and your process.

Be yourself, authentically you. If you love to dance in the rain, do it. I have participated in dancing in the grocery store to some great music more than once. My most recent impromptu dancing in the yogurt section brought a conversation about blues music and just feeling great from the beat. The couple next to me was smiling when we parted ways.

Here's a very important pro-tip: **don't take yourself too seriously**. Really, it's a key to good health, balancing the wave of feelings that can crop up in any situation, and it keeps us humble.

Write about a time when you took yourself too seriously — what happened and what were the consequences?

Now, write about a time when you didn't take yourself so seriously, compare your feelings and the lasting effect.

Take a look at what you wrote as your evolving areas, do any include **accepting yourself in different situations** or different experiences? Remember, give yourself grace and the space to learn about yourself, too.

What's one thing you might do that shows self-acceptance?

Do a body scan, how does your body feel?

Do a feelings scan, what are you feeling and what are your secondary feelings?

Do a mindfulness scan, in what way are you noticing yourself?

Do a spirituality scan, how present do you feel?

Do a work/school/legal/financial scan, how well are these areas in order?

Do a volition scan, what are your most recent decisions and how are you experiencing them?

Do an overall scan of the work you've done in this book, what have you gained from it?

What have you been able to let go?

What do you feel joyful about keeping and how are you **living** that thing?

What are your action plans in all the life areas, take time to review them, and where are you in the process of these?

Make your intentional list here, add goals and dates and specific language—

Chapter Eleven

What's in the Works?

Oh yes, there's more to the journey ahead!

THANK YOU FOR PURCHASING this book, I hope you've found many insights and you've committed to using the tools that fit for your journey.

This book is a labor of love, I want to produce options for a pathway to making healthy decisions and wellness practices for readers, and I hope that I've delivered.

I've mentioned oh so many resources and it's difficult to stop where I have because there are incredible writers and professionals out there — I hope you will follow up on the links and references I've included, again, the ones that fit best for you, because they offer **new levels of insight if you seek it.**

As for me, I have two (at least) projects in the works, please keep me in mind and check in for updates on my website and where ever you get books.

As I mentioned in the Introduction, I am open to feedback and corrections, if you noticed something in this book that you believe you'd like to comment on, please send me an email at: wbochoice@gmail.com

I also welcome hearing about your journey, how you went about the various steps and tools in this book, your **GO.BE.DO.** activities or other growth areas you'd like to share. With invitations like this there comes email volume, I may not be able to respond in a timely manner, yet I will make an effort. Questions about professional use of this book and its contents should be sent directly to me.

My website is **wellbeingone.net**, please take a look and engage in feedback on the blog. Additionally, you can find resources as well as book signing dates and IBL + Discovery Pathway at conferences and other events. Consultancy and public speaking are also part of my practice, if you'd like more information please contact me at: wbochoice@gmail.com

For now, I'll sign off, and I'm very much looking forward to our next meeting.

Here's to being choiceful — Keri